I'm Too Human to be Like Jesus

by Poppy Smith

DEDICATION

To Jim, God's gift to me.

CONTENTS

.

ONE

Is Growing Only for "Super-Saints"?

"THIS WOMAN CAN'T BE FOR REAL," I MUTTERED UNDER MY breath.

Standing serenely at the front of the church auditorium in the sweltering heat, a slender, beautifully dressed and made-up southern belle waited for the crowd of chattering women to quiet down. Not a drop of glistening sweat rolled down her face.

Since moving to Singapore (more accurately called "Sauna-pore") a few months earlier, where my husband had taken a new job, I had yet to achieve the "sweatless" look. Instead, my hair stuck like spaghetti strands to my forehead, my nose dripped (on the outside), and my skirt automatically shrink-wrapped itself to the back of my thighs whenever I sat down.

"Now girls," the object of my amazement called out, smiling angelically, "let's all focus on why we're here. We'll begin our time of worship by singing 'Great Is Thy Faithfulness.'"

Dutifully, I opened my hymnbook and began to sing with the rest. After all, who dared defy this model of perfection?

As the morning unfolded, my awe and envy expanded like a balloon filling with helium. Perched on the edge of my pew, I watched every move, listened to every word, caught every tone. And, amid my rapidly evaporating self-confidence, I reluctantly discovered that this woman was not only outwardly attractive, she was also spiritually gifted, mature, and genuinely warm.

I wish I were like her, I brooded to myself later in the day. *She seems so perfect. Imagine having hair that stands up nice and perky instead of flopping over and playing dead! And how does she radiate such coolness and serenity, while I'm constantly swiping at my red, perspiring face?*

She's flawless inside and out, I mused. *She knows the Word, prays without stumbling, and seems so spiritually all-together. It's as if she's strolling through life in a bubble of blessing.*

Have you ever met a woman like this? Ever had thoughts like this? Ever compared yourself to someone you perceived to be perfect and concluded you didn't measure up? Maybe you, too, wonder if growing spiritually strong is only for "super-saints" who have themselves and their lives under control. Being in the company of sweet-tempered women—women who are filled with faith, easily self-disciplined, and oozing with love for God and others—can make the rest of us want to slink away and hide.

Maybe what gets you down isn't the apparent perfection of others, but your own imperfections, which, you are convinced, must surely be obvious to everyone. Sliding your flaws and failings under the high-powered microscope of your critical inner self, perhaps you find yourself sighing, as I do, *I wish I were ... a lot that I'm not.* Or questioning, *Doesn't anybody else struggle like me?*

What is it that we wish we were? What struggles do we wish we could stomp right out of our lives? Your list might be long, but here are some common longings. See if you can identify with any of them.

I Wish I Were More ...

* *Patient.* "Why did I blast my horn at that white-haired lady doing forty-five miles an hour on the freeway?" you berate yourself. "She was concentrating so hard I must have made her jump out of her skin. Good grief, someday that could be me."

Or you groan, "I shouldn't have snatched that toy out of Jenny's hand when she didn't put it away quickly enough. And yesterday I was so impatient I shoved her arm in her coat because she was dawdling. What kind of mother am I, anyway?"

* *Self-controlled.* "I really couldn't help myself," you try to explain to your boggle-eyed spouse when the bills roll in. "I know my closet is full of shoes and my dresser lined with perfume bottles, but there's always something new out there! I can't help it if they keep filling the shops with new, appealing things."

Maybe you wonder when you'll learn to control your tongue and your temper. "I didn't need to unload my frustrations on that poor office manager," you reflect. "I could have chosen my words more carefully. No wonder people seem nervous when I'm around them."

* *Considerate.* Your mouth waters for the fresh strawberry pie buried under mounds of whipped cream. When it is served to your group crowded around the restaurant table, you manage, with a little effort, to get the biggest piece. Your husband, who is twice your size, gets the smallest piece, and gives you an unmistakable look. You ignore him. Later you somewhat guiltily admit, "I enjoyed every bite, but I guess I could have shared some with you." He gives you another look.

The parking lot was crowded. Your friend raved about the fantastic sale, but you knew your lunch break was too short to do it justice. Still, you couldn't resist going. Just then you spied a car backing out of a parking space. Zooming up in your little Honda as close as you dared, you noticed out of the corner of your eye another car clearly waiting for the empty spot. What should you do? Why, drive right in, jerk to a halt, avoid eye contact with the other driver, and bolt for the store door, of course. After all, what else could you do?

* *Kind.* You're torn as you think to yourself: *I know Sally needs support. I should be kind and help her, but that will mean taking care of her two out-of-control kids all day. I just can't face it.*

3

They'll tear up the house, eat what groceries I have left, and give me a major migraine. Maybe I'll go somewhere with my kids so I won't be here if she calls.

Your friend, who is single, tells you she is sick. You'd really like to go over and be the loving, Christian friend she needs, but you just have to get a project finished that's been hanging around for ages. The next day, when she tells you a colleague from work came over that evening with homemade soup, guilt engulfs you.

* *Organized/disciplined/spiritually "with it."* You really do want to pray like Praying Hyde (you know his name and it's obvious what he's famous for, but *who is he?*)— you promise sincerely that you'll pray for all sorts of people, and your list could be as long as your arm if you had only written down what they said. You wish you could remember where you put that verse you were going to memorize—and where was it you left off in your Bible reading? Wasn't it in Hezekiah somewhere? "If only God had made me like those 'super-saints,'" you mutter, "I could be doing all sorts of things for Him."

Recognize yourself yet? Check out a few more possibilities. This time we'll phrase it a little differently:

I Wish I Weren't So ...

* *Concerned with what others think of me.* You know that what others think about you isn't necessarily true, but you find yourself stewing over how a friend or co-worker views you. Your mother's opinion still affects your self-image—and here you are with kids of your own!

You can't help but notice that you don't have as much money or as nice a house as many people in your church, and you wonder, *Maybe we shouldn't invite newcomers over to our house. They might feel uncomfortable with our worn furniture and carpet.*

* *Manipulative*. You find it hard not to be in charge, either up front or behind the scenes. After all, you've had so much experience and know what needs to be done for the best. You also know how to get the praise and admiration you crave. You wish it weren't so, but deep down you recognize your insecurity and your need to control.

* *Worried about everything.* You can't stand those people who smile serenely, and say, "Don't worry about anything, just pray." You know they mean well, and that the apostle Paul said the same thing, but be realistic! How can you not worry when you've got a huge mortgage, two teenagers with raging hormones, and a husband starting to wear gold chains and eyeing little red sports cars?

And so our list goes on and on. I wish I were ... I wish I weren't ... I wish I were ... I wish I weren't ...

Take a moment and ask yourself: *What is it that I wish I were or weren't?*

If something jumps into your mind write it down.

The fact is, most of us can think of something, because who lives without flaws and failings? None of us do—because we are all human.

When I Blow It, I Feel ...

Stuffed in the aisle seat on a packed flight from Portland to Chicago, I grabbed my book and resolutely ignored the two women seated beside me. Newly acquainted, they chatted away with each other as if they were long-lost friends.

My natural inclination when pressed next to strangers is to go into my "reserved English-upbringing" mode. With head down, eyes glued to the page, my body language shouts loud and clear, "Leave me alone. I don't want to talk."

And so I remained for the whole trip—until twenty minutes before we landed.

"I'm taking a religion class at college," declared the young woman seated beside me to her new friend in the window seat. "Somebody was talking about being born-again, but I didn't know what they meant. Do you?" she inquired. Her companion had no idea. And I didn't dare say anything after my deliberate lack of friendliness!

I knew I had blown it. *What kind of a Christian am I?* I silently groaned. Feeling like an utter failure, I wondered how God could continue to use me—or bless me. I had shown a lack of love, a lack of availability to God, and even a lack of courtesy. I felt awful.

Ever been there? Don't give up. God *is* at work in us in spite of our failures!

Our responses to blowing it can be as varied as our personalities. See if you recognize any of the following reactions.

Depression, despair, self-condemnation: "What's the matter with me?" Marcie choked out to God as she lay on her bed staring at the ceiling. "I want to please You and be a loving, positive mother, but I blow it constantly. I tried to be patient and understanding with Jamie, but his attitude and laziness irritated me so much. I didn't mean to call him names, but they just came out of my mouth. God, I'm so sorry. I feel like such a failure."

Defiance, anger, helplessness: "God, how can You expect me to act like Jesus?" Ellen demanded angrily. "Did He have to work with a group as incompetent as this one? It's impossible to be gentle and loving when people are so difficult."

Detachment, apathy, self-pity: "I've given up trying," said Holly. "I know I'm supposed to accept everyone, but the way I was raised taught me that some people are more important than others, even worth more. I guess I will always be that way. I'll never be what

God wants me to be, but I know He loves me anyway, so why bother trying to be something I'm not? I'm just me, warts and all."

You're not alone if you struggle with these common reactions to a sense of failure—depression, defiance, detachment. In fact, you might have an even stronger response—angrily questioning God, asking Him why He gave you such impossibly high standards to live by. Or, overcome by a mixture of frustration and helplessness, you may cry out, "God, do You know what You're asking when You say don't worry, love your enemies, and forgive those who have deeply wounded you? It's impossible! I don't have it in me. How can I ever please You?"

Apathy is another response—often hiding deep-seated resentment against God. It's a form of coping. You shrug your shoulders, wish spiritual transformation were possible but, being realistic, adopt the "I've tried it; I can't change, why bother?" syndrome.

Think about how you feel when you try and fail. What do you tell yourself? What impact does this have on your emotional and spiritual well-being? Write down what comes to mind.

Is There Hope?

After many experiences of trying and failing to be more like Christ, it's legitimate to ask if non-"super-saints" like us can change. Can we, who maybe battle short tempers, fight feelings of discouragement, shy away from caring about others, and only daydream about a disciplined life ever be any different? Can we grow spiritually strong in spite of feelings that run amok, flaws that seem as ingrown as toenails, and failures that pit the landscapes of our lives? Is there hope for those of us who can't achieve super-sainthood? Is there hope for me? What about you?

Despite what you or I feel about our frustratingly slow, bumbling around, falling down, picking-ourselves-back-up pace of spiritual progress, the answer is most definitely YES! How do I know?

Well, stop and think of all the men and women in Scripture used by God. None began as a spiritual giant. All were fallible; some made atrocious mistakes. Yet eventually they matured, grew, developed a strong faith in God, and served Him in a multitude of ways.

Let's Look at Some of These People:

Rahab. She easily comes to mind. A Canaanite prostitute from the city of Jericho, Rahab knew nothing about the one true God until she heard of the miraculous deliverance of the Jews from Egypt. Because of her belief in the Lord God of heaven, she risked her life to save two Israelite spies. As a result, Rahab and her family were saved from the destruction of Jericho and became part of the Israelite nation. Rahab not only changed her lifestyle, she also changed her beliefs. And because of God's endless love and transforming work in her life, her name is mentioned in the genealogy of both David and Jesus (Matthew 1:5).

Esther. Coming from a totally different background, Esther is another woman mightily used of God. Raised in a sheltered, devout Jewish home, Esther was taken into the palace of the king of Persia for his sensual pleasure. After she became queen, the Jewish people faced a threat of imminent extermination. Mordecai, Esther's cousin, urged her to go to the king and plead for their people. In essence, her response was "You're crazy, Mordecai. Don't tell me to go into the king's presence uninvited—that will get me killed! You can't expect me to risk my life." But in the end she agreed, becoming God's instrument at that time for saving His people from extinction. Did she start out as a "super-saint," filled with courage and faith in God? Not at all. She was scared silly, like many of us would be. (See Esther 2-7.)

The Samaritan woman. With a sexual past similar to some women today, the Samaritan woman would never be mistaken for an evangelist. Jesus turned their meeting at a well into an explanation

8

of the living water he offered. When Jesus changed her life, she ran to tell all the upright, moral folk back home to come and see a man who told her everything she ever did (John 4:7-30). Was she poor material for God to use? Yes, humanly speaking, but not from God's perspective. His joy is to forgive and transform lives, both then and now.

Martha. Let's look at another imperfect woman. Martha was a regular synagogue attender, faithful to God—but task-oriented, impatient, easily frustrated, a woman who tried to do too much and then would explode with exasperation when others didn't pitch in. Honored by the Lord for her service and hospitality, He nevertheless wanted to draw her into greater spiritual awareness of who He was. Standing outside Lazarus's tomb, He challenged her faith: "Did I not tell you that if you believed you would see the glory of God?" Struck by His forthright question, Martha rose above her practical, no-nonsense personality, allowed the stone to be removed, and saw her beloved brother come forth from the tomb (John 11:21-44).

Women, however, aren't the only sources of unlikely material God uses to mold and change. He chose some men who had their share of struggles, too:

Moses. Who was God's hand-picked person to lead the Israelites out of Egypt? Moses. Whining, scared, stubborn Moses! Was he a "super-saint"? Not by any stretch. Did he grow and become spiritually strong in spite of his trip-ups, blow-ups, and hang-ups? Absolutely (Exodus 3-4:17).

Peter. Move ahead thousands of years and recall who loved the Lord deeply and vowed he'd never let Him down. Remember Peter? Remember his stumbling and bumbling? His foot-in-mouth disease? No one but Jesus saw the potential behind his warm, tripping all over, eager-puppy personality.

Denying His Lord after all his bold declarations of eternal faithfulness, Peter must have felt that their relationship was over— he had sunk as low as he could go. Yet a short while later, Jesus turned to him and said three times, "Feed my sheep" (John 21:15-19). Why? Why didn't the Lord reject Peter? Because He knew what Peter could become, despite his flaws and failures. And the Lord is right about our potential for spiritual growth also, because He is the One who puts within us both the desire and the power for such a change to take place.

Growth Is God's Idea

Plop! Malaika, my firstborn, collapsed on her diaper-padded bottom wailing in frustration.

"Come on, sweetheart," I entreated, "try again. You're a big girl now. Look, you can almost walk."

Crawling to the edge of the sofa, Malaika pulled herself up, her face creased in a wide smile of excitement and anticipation. Slowly letting go of her anchor, she eyed the vast distance to the other side of the room, chuckled with delight, and staggered forward a few more steps. Plop! Down she went again.

"You're nearly there!" I cried, scooping her up with a big hug and a kiss. "Soon you're going to be walking all by your self. You're such a clever girl."

Beaming with delight, I watched Malaika try again and again to master this new step of growth. No matter how many times she tumbled over, scraped herself, cried with frustration, or shed tears of pain, she had to attempt to walk. Why? Because God has created human beings with the drive to grow, to develop, to mature physically.

The same is true of us spiritually. Every urge we have to pray, to help someone else, to give time or money or energy to serving Christ, is implanted by God. God is at work in us to conform us to the image of His Son. And God is delighted by every effort we make toward that goal. Sometimes, however, we have our own ideas about how to grow spiritually strong.

I Can Do It—Just Tell Me How

"I don't want to be just an ordinary Christian," Joanie said to her friend Shannon who had shown her the way to faith in Christ. "I want to be a really good Christian. Please tell me what I should do," she continued. "When should I get up in the morning to pray? How long should I read my Bible? What else is necessary?"

Alarm bells went off in Shannon's head. With a quick prayer for wisdom, she plunged in to teach this new believer a basic truth of spiritual growth so many miss.

"Joanie, it's wonderful you want to develop your new relationship with God," she responded carefully, "but loving God and being loved by Him isn't about keeping a list of requirements. God loves you fully right now. Spending time in prayer and studying His Word isn't going to make Him love you more. What it will do, though, is increase *your* love and knowledge of Him."

I Must Do It

Believing that our performance of religious rites will win us God's favor—and that failing to keep up a daily routine of required spiritual exercises will bring God's disfavor—is a common fallacy. Coming from a culture, home, or deeply entrenched belief that performance, achievement, and success are the only paths to acceptance and approval can skew our understanding of spiritual growth.

Our thinking often goes something like this: *Surely if I'm a good Christian and do everything I think God requires of me, I'll not only succeed in life but I'll also earn His blessing and approval.* That's false thinking. God doesn't put us into categories of "saints" and "super-saints," dropping blessings on us according to how successful we are at keeping our imagined list of divinely required behaviors.

Believing God rewards performance can drive a high achiever to frenzied levels of unhealthy commitments. Molly takes my breath away. Teaching at a community college two evenings a week, she also leads two women's groups during the week, teaches Sunday school with her husband, attends a home fellowship, hosts groups at her home, and is studying for her Ph.D. All at the same time.

Kathleen, who battles perfectionism and workaholism, writes out daily, weekly, and monthly spiritual goals. Should she get sick for a day or be sidetracked by unexpected circumstances, what would happen? Would she rest and rejoice in God's love and acceptance even if she couldn't keep up with her self-imposed spiritual routine? Or is it more likely that she'd be plagued by guilt because she'd see herself as having failed to please God? And, if she should meet all her goals, who would receive the praise?

Believing God rewards performance also affects women who don't fit the above category. Instead of frantically cranking up the level of spiritual activities and exercises, would-be "super-saints" are tempted to give up all efforts to grow. Sighing with discouragement they ask, *What's the use? How will I ever experience God's blessing when I can't even pray two days in a row?*

So just what is the truth? What does God say about performance and failure to perform? Paul answers this question in his letter to the Galatians, who were struggling with this same issue. Galatians 3:3 says, "Are you so foolish? After beginning with the Spirit, are you now trying to attain your goal by human effort?" Keeping self-imposed rules or striving to measure up to the expectations of other Christians won't earn you God's blessing, nor can it earn your salvation.

You might know this truth, but nevertheless, take a moment and reflect on the spiritual standards by which you measure yourself. What are they?

Why are these standards important to you? Be honest.

God, You Do It Without Me

Much as we might wish it were true, growth doesn't come by the opposite extreme, either. Waiting passively for God to wave a magic wand over you and pronounce, "You're changed!" is like kissing a frog and expecting it to materialize into the man of your dreams. You're not likely to be zapped by an instant, character-transforming lightning bolt from heaven. God doesn't remove our sinful desires, attitudes, or behavior apart from willing involvement on our part. That isn't His way of working. How well I know.

When Jim, my husband, finished his surgical training, we didn't have much money. In his first years in practice the money he brought home covered the mortgage, food, and a car. After tithing, precious little was left, certainly not enough for the new wallpaper I craved, or the furniture I looked at longingly. Being home every day with two small children gave me plenty of time to look at what I had—and I didn't like it.

Showing Jim picture after picture of decorator-designed rooms in magazines didn't help. "We don't have the money" was always his response. And like all down-to-earth, sensible men, he added, "I know our furniture isn't fancy but it's serviceable. The sofa will probably last another ten years."

But my desire for new furniture, new wallpaper—even a new house—didn't go away. How could it, when I was feeding my cravings and my discontent with trips to the mall, furniture stores, one-stop decorator shops, and designer boutiques?

"Dear God," I'd pray, "please change Jim's mind. Couldn't You make him willing to put it on Visa since we don't have the cash?" Did God answer my prayer? Of course. I got an answer. Just not the one I was looking for.

The Holy Spirit impressed on my mind: *Poppy, you need to change your focus. By feasting your eyes on all the things you can't have, you fill your heart with discontent and unhappiness. Let me touch this area of your life. I want you to experience freedom from the love of things, which dominates your mind and determines your moods.*

Change is hard work! No wonder we wish God would wave a magic wand and, without any self-denial or discipline on our part, accomplish His purposes in us. Life would be so much easier if God would heed Nike's slogan: *Just do it!* But that isn't how He works. God is not a genie in a bottle who responds to our commands. He instructs us what to do through His Word and provides the power to change through His Holy Spirit, but then He tells *us* to work out our salvation. In other words, He says, "Act on what I've revealed to you." When God tells us to "just do it," He gives a heavenly command.

I could have waited the rest of my life for God to miraculously change my grumbling and discontented attitude. But if I had done nothing to cooperate with the process, nothing would have happened. And I would have become bitter and disillusioned with God.

Here I Am, Lord—Please Work in Me

Inner growth doesn't come by lengthening our list of "things I have to do to feel accepted by God." Other people might be impressed, but if we're operating in our own energy, all our efforts will amount to nothing. On the other hand, nothing will change in our lives by passively waiting for God to turn us into instant "super-saints."

So what *should* we do? Before change can occur we must ask God for His help. He wants to build in us a hunger to please Him, a willingness to hear what He is saying, and an eagerness to obey what He shows us.

What did I need to do when God convicted me of my grumbling and complaining spirit about our ugly wallpaper and furniture? Once I decided it was time to let God change me, He impressed me with three practical steps: they involved my mind, my mouth, and my use of time.

1. *My mind.* If I found myself daydreaming about sofas, draperies, and beautiful rooms, I needed to practice Romans 12:2: "Do not conform any longer to the pattern of this world, but be transformed by the renewing of your mind." Focusing my mind on Scripture verses about contentment and acknowledging God's provision of a roof over our heads and clothes to wear helped. So did rearranging what furniture we had. My ability to push and shove heavy pieces of furniture around the house never ceased to astound Jim. What can I say? When you're desperate, strength comes from somewhere!

2. *My mouth.* When I opened my mouth to complain about my kitchen's outdated Early American coffeepot-print wallpaper, I was to close it—my mouth, that is. What an amazingly simple yet effective strategy! Learning to thank God and Jim for what we did have took me another step in the right direction.

3. *My use of time.* Knowing that browsing through furniture stores and gazing longingly at expensive decorator magazines only made me more miserable and discontented, I needed to quit cold turkey. After all, my chances of having furniture featured in *Lifestyles of the Rich and Famous* were quite remote. So why keep torturing myself?

Did this three-pronged approach work? Yes—when I applied it, and it still does.

The central purpose of this book is to help you open up your life to God's working. In theological terms, this process of being changed into the likeness of Jesus is called "sanctification." That's what we're going to explore here, chapter by chapter. The wonderful things God has done for us, and what He will yet do as we continue to walk with Him, hopefully will become clear. We'll look at what it means to grow in faith, trust, perseverance, and peace—and expect a few surprises, such as what He expects *us* to do, because we certainly have a role to play in our own spiritual development.

For now, let's make a start. Is there an area in your life that needs attention? It can be something small or something large. Write it down (use code language if you're afraid someone besides God might see it).

How willing are you to let God remake an area in your life? Jot down your answer, but take a moment to talk to God honestly about how you feel—and ask Him to build spiritual hunger in you.

Now think about the following. What small, immediate changes can you make in these specific areas for growth to occur in your life?

Your mind:

Your mouth:

Your use of time:

Other areas:

God's goal is not to make you fret and fume over your inability to be perfect in every way. Nor does He secretly delight in causing you misery and stress in your attempts to grow spiritually. Like a loving parent watching his child's stumbling attempts to walk, so God sees our efforts. He knows, as does any parent, that we will fall. Yet patiently, lovingly, He lifts us up again and again. He knows we are learning a whole new way to live. Failure is part of the learning process.

But failure isn't the end of the story. What is God's will? That every believer experience progressive change (1 Thessalonians 4:1-3a). Transformation of who we are on the inside and how we act on the outside takes time. In fact, the process lasts for a lifetime. But you *can* actually see change taking place when those responses and behaviors in you that aren't "like Christ" diminish and those that are increase. Others will also see it.

Tim, a friend who attended our church and was a member of our home Bible study many years ago, encouraged me more than he knew one night. Leaving our home, he turned to me and said, "You have really changed." What a thrill! Knowing I needed a major renovation by the Holy Spirit, I had been praying and cooperating with God as best I knew how. When someone said, "It's noticeable," I felt as if God had reached down and given me a big hug.

If you feel like a failure in some area of your life, you're at the perfect place to begin today to grow spiritually strong. Knowing you're not a "super-saint" puts you and me exactly where we need to be—ready to listen, learn, and apply whatever the Spirit of God is telling us.

As you move through each chapter, ask God to reignite your desire to grow and to encourage you in exactly the areas you need. Then, as you begin to do what He shows you, watch for change—and give Him the credit.

Spiritual growth isn't just for "super-saints," those all-together people who seem so far removed from our human ups-and-downs. This joy is for all of us, regardless of our trip-ups, blow-ups, and hang-ups.

In your quest to grow spiritually strong, have you ever sighed, *How can I be more like you, Lord?* I certainly have. How can it happen? What do we need to know? Is there something we need to do? Let's find out.

Reflections—for Thought and Discussion

1. What comes to mind when you think of a "super-saint"? How do you feel when you're around someone like this?

2. What do you wish you were: more patient, self-controlled, considerate, kind.... What do you wish you weren't? Why?

3. How do you react when you blow it? What encouragement do you find in the fact that God always works with imperfect people?

4. How do you honestly feel about measuring up to your ideal of a Christian? Write down all the facts you find in the following verses: Romans 4:7-8; 5:1-2, 6, 9-10; 8:33-39. How could believing these affect your feelings about God's acceptance of you?

5. Since becoming a Christian, what specific changes have you seen in an attitude, behavior, or thinking pattern?

6. Are there more changes you would like God to work in you? What step could you take this week in your home, church, or workplace to cooperate with Him in this?

Memory Verse

"Therefore, there is now no condemnation for those who are in Christ Jesus" (Romans 8:1).

TWO

How Can I Be More Like You, Lord?

"THE MORE YOU LAUGH AT HIM, THE LONGER HE'LL ACT SILLY," my husband said quietly.

"But he's so funny," I replied, "I can't help it." I worked hard to smother my laughter at the antics of a little Chinese boy sitting beside Jim in the hospital reception area.

Waiting for some friends to arrive for a tour of the hospital in Singapore where he works, Jim was trying to catch a quick nap, while I watched the nonstop activity of our tiny neighbor. After jumping up and over the rows of armchairs, he ran to the wall-length window, tapping on it loudly. People waiting outside for a taxi turned around, startled. With a grin at his newfound audience, he charged around the reception area, arms outstretched, pretending to be an airplane. Then he spotted Jim.

Sitting with one leg crossed over the other, his head propped up by his hand, Jim's six-foot, five-inch frame was hard to miss. Fascinated by this huge foreigner, the boy studied him. Within a few seconds, he slid into the seat next to Jim, crossed one leg over the other, and carefully propped up his head in an identical manner. He then peered up to see if Jim had noticed. It was too much for me—I burst out laughing all over again.

Even though the differences between a six-foot-plus American man and a Chinese preschooler couldn't possibly be bridged, this little mischief made an all-out effort. Having observed Jim carefully, he mimicked him to a "t."

Children imitate adults—usually their parents. Watching silently and sweetly (sometimes), they don't miss a word or gesture. Like spies in our own camp, they observe what we do and how we respond to situations. This has an uncanny effect. Try listening in when your child is playing. *No, you can't do that. Do you hear me? Mommy said NO!* It's your own voice, words, and inflections. It's scary. They take in more than we can imagine. They often become clones of *us*.

If only it were that simple to imitate Jesus. The apostle Paul said, "Imitate me, even as I imitate Christ." But what did he mean? Are we to grit our teeth and tell ourselves before the day begins, "Now, be like Jesus. He was kind, always giving time and attention to others, feeding thousands, tending the sick, giving wise counsel to all. You're supposed to be like Him, so no slacking off and taking it easy." Are you eager to experience burnout and disillusionment? A sure way is to try to imitate Christ by your own efforts.

Yet we are to imitate Him, to be like Him, to reflect clearly our relationship with Him. But how is it possible when He was without sin, unlike all the rest of us? How can we be more like Him in our character, behavior, and attitudes? To respond to people as He did? And exactly how does the Holy Spirit answer our pleadings to be more like the Lord? Have you wrestled with these questions? I have.

When you ask God questions from the heart, stay alert for His answers. Help is on the way. On one occasion, God used the Christian classic Hannah Hurnard's *Hind's Feet on High Places* to help me understand how He works in our lives.[1] The book is an allegory about a young girl called Much Afraid. Feeling trapped by her aunt and cousins, the Fearing family, she longed to escape and live on the high places with the Good Shepherd. But she despaired that it could ever happen because she was born with crippled feet and a crooked mouth. How could she, with all her imperfections, possibly hope to share the intimate company of the Good Shepherd and his followers in the flower-dappled, alpine meadows high above the valley?

As a young Christian struggling with wanting to grow more like the Lord, I strongly identified with Much Afraid's despair. My physical feet were in fine shape, but my spiritual feet seemed to constantly trip over whatever loomed in front of me. Relatives, husband, small children, little money, loneliness, frustration—it didn't matter. Far from leaping gracefully from mountain peak to mountain peak, I staggered about in the depths of failure, wondering how I'd ever get out of the miry clay I was stuck in.

As for my mouth—oh, it wasn't crooked in appearance, but it didn't smile warmly or spout comforting Scripture verses. When my emotions asserted themselves, like bursts of volcanic activity, I spewed angry accusations, resentful feelings, or tearful "poor-me" diatribes. I felt my chances of ever being remotely like Jesus were about as likely as my scaling Mount Everest. Despite all the promises of Scripture that we can reign in life over sin, that the truth sets us free, and that Christ came to give abundant life, all I could see before me was a lifetime of sighing, *Will I ever be any different?*

In answer to my despair, I'd like to say God showed me some snappy, quick-fix solutions I could now pass on to you. But nothing like that happened. What I did discover is that I can't live the Christian life by myself—and God never meant that I try. Nor can you. That's why He sent Christ, with all His resources, to live in us.

Living in us, the Spirit of Christ encourages, teaches, convicts, and enables believers to do His will. This means that as we grow in our knowledge of God and His Word, believe that it's true, and obey what the Holy Spirit impresses upon us, change does occur. Instead of our saying, "I just can't (or won't, or don't want to) do that," the Spirit gives us the power we need in every situation. He *can* enable us to apologize for an unkind remark, speak the truth when it's not easy, turn off a trashy TV program, or resist the urge to gossip.

Truth Transforms

Growing more like the Lord begins with realizing that He lives in us—in fact, our bodies are His temple or dwelling place (1 Corinthians 6:19). Describing himself as knocking at the door of our hearts, Jesus promises that if we open the door from the inside, He will come in and fellowship with us (Revelation 3:20). This doesn't occur only when we first come to know God. It's a permanent union made possible by His death for our sins. When we place our faith in Christ, we are not only washed clean of our sins, Christ comes into our hearts once and for all.

So here we are knowing that something astonishing has happened but still trapped in the helpless feeling that we'll never become more like Jesus. How do we discover the key to living with joy and hope of change, shaking off despair and frustration? By finding out what the Bible says about this new, intimate relationship we've been given by God.

Like all spiritual truth, the mystery that "Christ lives in me," has to be rediscovered over and over in every area of our lives. Can we grasp what Christ accomplished at the Cross? Can we know that Christ lives in us? Yes, with His Spirit empowering us, we can.

Without a clear understanding of these teachings, it's too easy to give in to discouragement and succumb to Satan's whispers, *Why try? You'll never be any different. You'll never measure up and be like Jesus.* If our thoughts and feelings are not based on biblical truth but half-thoughtout ideas picked up here and there, we're vulnerable to the Enemy's lies.

Mary's experience illustrates this. "My friend Lilly and I attend a Bible study," she said. "One week we were discussing how Christians hear God's voice. Lilly, who hasn't studied the Bible much, spoke up and asked, 'Do I belong to God if I don't hear Him speak to me in an audible voice? After all, Jesus said whoever belongs to God hears what God says, and if we don't, it's because we don't belong to Him. I'm confused. Do I belong to God or don't I?' Several others in the group looked just as puzzled," Mary added.

Have you ever found yourself wondering about where you stand with God? It's a common experience that's solved only by having an accurate understanding of what God did at the time of our salvation, and is continuing to do today. Knowing these truths frees us from thinking it's all over with God any time we blow it, or worrying that we'll be rejected because we haven't heard audible voices. Being sure of these truths is essential for spiritual and emotional stability; learning to trust God's grace is part of the process.

What are some of these truths that inspire us to believe we can experience a growing love relationship with God? Let's focus on four stupendous New Testament teachings that provide assurance and hope.

• *You're a New Person*

• *You're "in Christ"*

• *You're a "Saint"*

• *You're Empowered by the Holy Spirit*

You're a New Person

In various letters to the early church, Paul repeated over and over a life-changing truth. He joyfully declared, "Our old self was crucified with him" (Romans 6:6). "If anyone is in Christ, he is a new creation; the old has gone, the new has come!" (2 Corinthians 5:17). "You were once darkness, but now you are light in the Lord" (Ephesians 5:8).

Scripture teaches that we are not who we once were, so we need never say, "I'm no different than before." You *are* different—even though you might not have seen as much change as you'd like. Keep saying yes to God and more change will appear. Naturally, we'd love it if these statements meant we became perfect in an instant and that all our past programming and responses had been deleted by the push of a button. But if this were so, what about those of us who are only too aware of our failure to live up to perfection? But something did happen at the time of our new birth. What was it and what difference does it make today?

You Had a New Birth

Do you remember your first birth—the bright lights, masked faces, and how you yelled when the doctor slapped your bottom? Of course you don't. You couldn't possibly comprehend what was happening on that momentous occasion. No doubt years passed before you found out about the birds and the bees, how babies grow in their mommy's tummy, how they come out, and other mysteries of the birth process.

What's the spiritual parallel? As in our physical birth, we probably had no idea what was really happening when we were reborn spiritually. When it happened to me, I didn't know anything beyond the basics: Jesus died on the Cross for me; God forgave my sins when I believed this; God loves me; and I am now in His family. I knew something happened to me when I was born spiritually because I felt release from guilt, I was flooded with peace, and I desired to know more about God. But all I understood was what had happened *in me*.

You Have a New Identity

Many years later, however, I began to learn what occurred at my spiritual birth from God's perspective: He brought me into a totally new relationship with Him, which changed the way He will deal with me forever. I'm no longer an alien with no claims on God. I'm now a citizen of heaven.

Drawing up a will, our lawyer warned me, "Should Jim precede you in death and you're not a United States citizen, Poppy, you will lose considerable tax benefits." *Finally*, I thought. *A good reason to become a U.S. citizen.*

After living twenty-five years in America, I still felt extremely reluctant to change my citizenship. My British passport represented one of the few remaining links with the land of my birth. But the time had obviously come. Putting aside the emotional impact of such a decision, I knew I needed to look after my financial well-being should I become a widow. "Okay," I conceded. "To keep the government from taking Jim's hard-earned money or forcing me to flee, cash in hand, the day after his funeral, I'll do it."

What changed in my relationship with the United States government? I can vote, of course, but there's more. Now that I'm a citizen, the government is responsible to warn me about various dangers and rescue me from all sorts of deadly perils. Before, when I was merely a permanent resident, facing deadly perils was my problem. Having no claim on governmental help, I would have to manage the best I could. Now, because I legally belong, I have a whole new relationship with the United States of America. I'm part of it.

In somewhat the same way, because of Christ, we also have a whole new relationship with God. He now calls us His own. We belong to Him and He willingly undertakes to care for us, rescuing us from spiritual perils—even when we have no one to blame but ourselves for some of the trouble we get into.

You Have a New Relationship

At the same time that our standing with God changed, He gave us a new heart capable of hearing His voice and responding in loving obedience.

Much as we wish it were so, our new birth didn't instantly change us into fully mature disciples of Christ. We were born immature, floundering babies, totally dependent. Fortunately for us, God knew how much help we needed. In fact, before each of us became His child, He had already planned how he would bring about His purposes in us.

What, then, does it mean to be a new person? Ephesians 2:4-5 states, "Because of his great love for us, God, who is rich in mercy, made us alive with Christ even when we were dead in transgressions—it is by grace you have been saved." Astounding, isn't it? We are in a new relationship with God— no longer sinners facing His righteous judgment but profoundly loved and precious children, those whom He has forgiven and calls His own. Because Christ bore our sin, our standing in God's eyes is forever radically altered.

When I began to grasp the magnitude of God's love and unconditional acceptance, I wanted to cry, jump in the air, and click my heels with excitement all at the same time. I did cry, and still do quite often when I think about God's love.

Knowing who you are in God's eyes makes a tremendous difference in how you view your relationship with Him.

"When I blew it before," recounted Julia, "I used to call myself names, telling myself what a useless Christian I was and how could God ever love and accept me. I inflicted all this misery on myself for several days because I wanted to show God how sorry I was. Then I'd come crawling on my knees begging Him to forgive me.

"Now, when I trip over my flaws and failures, or even fall flat on my face, I know God is waiting for me to come to Him in repentance, just as before. But—He is not standing with His arms crossed (so to speak), frowning, and checking His list to see how many times I've committed the same sin. No. Like the father of the prodigal son, He is looking for me to come home to Him, longing to forgive, restore, and celebrate because this child who went her own way has come home."

Understanding that she belonged to God and was precious in His eyes no matter how she failed made Julia eager to come to Him for forgiveness and restoration of fellowship. "I don't want to wallow in guilt anymore," she said. "I know God wants me to come right away so nothing takes away my joy or blocks His working in my life. Instead of lugging around my usual backpack of guilt and misery, I feel light-hearted joy knowing God loves and accepts me with all my weaknesses. His grace is no longer an abstract doctrine to me, it is a living reality."

How about you? What are your thoughts about God, yourself, and your failures? To uncover what you honestly think, ask yourself the following:

How does God view me on my spiritually "good" days, according to my criteria? (Try to answer according to your innermost feelings, not what you know mentally.)

How do I feel God views me on my spiritually "bad" days? If there's a difference, what makes me think this is so?

You're "in Christ"

Have you noticed the phrase "in Christ" in the New Testament? Have you wondered what it means or how this can't-see-it-but-it's-real union happened, whereby Christ is in you and you are in Him? Is it all too mysterious and spiritual to grasp? Or is it better left to those "super-saints" who smile serenely, if a bit indulgently, and say, "Let me help you understand. It's like this...."

As a finite human being, I'm sure I'll never grasp all that it means to be "in Christ" or comprehend fully the depths of Christ in me. However, regardless of the degree to which we understand these truths, we're told that we have been blessed *in Christ*; there is no condemnation for those *in Christ*; and all who are *in Christ* will be made alive.

Statements declaring Christ is *in us* also abound. We're told that *Christ in us* is the hope of glory, He lives *in us*, and He abides *in us*.

Trying to grasp exactly what our union with Christ means is a bit like my experience of trying to understand electricity. "It's like this," explains my patient husband, "There's ..." All I hear is a blur of words that I can't quite make sense of. However, I know electricity exists, I need it, and I definitely benefit from it. In the larger sense, spiritual truths that are beyond our full, human understanding are the same.

In *Christian Theology*, author Willard Erickson endeavors to explain how our being "in Christ" affects our daily relationship with God. He writes, "When the Father evaluates or judges us before the law, he does not look upon us alone. We are in his sight one with Christ. God always sees the believer in union with Christ and he measures the two of them together."[2]

What's the result? When you shriek at your teenager, gossip about the boss, envy your friend's looks, house, and husband, God's hatred of sin doesn't pour over you in disgust and condemnation. Amazingly, He sees you incorporated in Christ whose perfection covers your sins and imperfections.

Don't imagine, however, that God has changed His view of sin. He hasn't. Because He is holy, He has an abiding, unchanging hatred of evil and therefore can never excuse it. How then can He love us day in and day out?

John Stott writes, "When we are united to Christ a mysterious exchange takes place: He took our curse, so that we may receive His blessing; He became sin with our sin, so that we may become righteous with His righteousness."[3] In God's eyes, the debt for all our sin and failure, both before we were saved and every day since, has been paid in full by His Son. God sees us now as united "in Christ."

Doesn't this excite you and make you want to dance with joy? Our relationship with God isn't based on our ability to be like Jesus twenty-four hours a day or to hear an audible voice. We are His because God chose to love us and draw us to himself. But there's more wonderful news.

You're a "Saint"

In addition to proclaiming that we're in a new relationship with God, the Bible gives us a new name. Believers are called "saints," people who are holy and righteous in His sight (Ephesians 1:1; Philippians 1:1). It all seems so preposterous from our viewpoint, but that's what God says.

The topic of how God views us cropped up at a women's Bible study and Sara expressed what most of us feel. "There's no way I'm a saint!" she exclaimed. "And I'm certainly not holy and righteous. I yelled at the kids in the back of the car to stop squabbling. I even threatened I'd make them get out and walk the rest of the way home. And I meant it. Be realistic. I'm no saint. Just ask my kids. Ask my husband!"

Do you feel the same way? You will if your view of being a saint is dependent on your feelings and failings rather than on God's declaration regarding your position in His eyes.

Paul didn't hesitate to call the early Christians "saints." Were they super-spiritual, free of flaws and failings, full of love for others, and overflowing with forgiveness for those who had harmed them? No. Listen to what Paul had to tell them: "Don't get drunk, deal with your jealousy and quarreling, speak truthfully, don't steal or be sexually immoral, and get rid of all bitterness, rage, and anger" (Ephesians 4-5 paraphrase). What a bunch to start the church with! Not one of them seemed in the least like the Lord. Yet Paul called these believers saints, dearly loved of God.

Position and Practice

If saints are not perfect people, what are they? What does God mean when He declares over two hundred times that believers are "saints," "holy ones," or "righteous ones"? All these terms speak of our position in God's eyes because we are "in Christ." They don't imply that we have achieved some level of spirituality that we know denies reality. It isn't our practice that qualifies us to be called saints. We are saints because we belong to Jesus Christ.

However, there's more to it than that. The root meaning of both "saint" and "sanctify" is "to set apart for a special purpose." In the Old Testament, God told the Israelites to sanctify themselves. The priests were told to do the same thing. And various articles used in worship were also to be sanctified. In the New Testament, the Lord said He sanctified (set apart) himself for the purpose of redemption. Christians are also called to set themselves apart to God, turning away from whatever dishonors His name and, instead, living lives that worship and serve Him. To be a saint, then, is a position we have by virtue of being in Christ. But God is concerned with far more than our status—He wants our conduct to reflect who we are. In His love and wisdom, He has provided what we need for this to happen—a power beyond ourselves.

You're Empowered by the Holy Spirit

The story is told of a group of American tourists visiting an ancient English village. As they trooped along, laden down with cameras, water bottles, and maps, they shook their heads in amazement at the one-thousand-year-old church and the three-hundred-year-old cottages. Convinced that the village had to be the birthplace of some famous person, one of them decided to find out. Just then he spotted a villager sitting on a bench puffing on a pipe, quietly watching them.

"Excuse me, sir," he said. "Would you mind telling me if any great person was born in this village?" After drawing a few puffs from his pipe and looking thoughtful, the villager responded: "Nope. Only babies."

All great men and women came into the world as helpless babies. So did all the spiritual greats that you and I look at and admire, those whose lives are characterized by Christlikeness and fruitful service for God.

All Christians begin their spiritual journey at the same place—as immature and struggling followers of Jesus. So how do some become spiritual greats? Do they have more brains than the rest of us, more dynamic personalities, good family connections? No, the secret of their spiritual effectiveness is found in their dependence on the power of the indwelling Spirit of God to work out God's purposes through them.

Hudson Taylor, an English missionary who pioneered work in China and founded the China Inland Mission (now Overseas Missionary Fellowship), discovered this truth and called it the "exchanged life." In describing the difference between constant struggle and failure, and trusting God to work in him through the Holy Spirit's indwelling power, he wrote:

31

How does the branch bear fruit? Not by incessant effort, nor vain struggles. It simply abides in the vine and fruit appears. How then shall a Christian bear fruit? Not by efforts and struggles ... but by focusing our thoughts and hearts on Christ; completely surrendering our whole being to Him and constantly looking to Him for grace.

Notice that when our minds and hearts are focused on Christ and our wills are completely surrendered to Him, the fruit of a changed life occurs. We don't have to grab ourselves by the scruff of the neck and grimly mutter, "Get a grip. You should read the Bible an hour a day and follow that by praying on your knees for all the lost and hurting people in the world; and never say no to any request to serve, even if you're already on five committees at church. After all, you've got to work for God and pay Him back for all He did for you." Following a religion like that is enough to make anyone run in the opposite direction.

How, then, do we bear spiritual fruit? By recognizing that Christ lives in us and because of this, our minds, hearts, and wills belong to Him. Paul referred to our part in bearing spiritual fruit when he said, "Set your hearts on things above ... set your minds on things above ... put to death, therefore, whatever belongs to your earthly nature" (Colossians 3:1-5).

David vibrantly illustrates how our mind, heart, and will are linked in the growth process. Turning his thoughts to God's glorious power, amazing love, and constant watch-care over us, David wrote, "When I consider your heavens, the work of your fingers, the moon and the stars, which you have set in place, what is man that you are mindful of him, the son of man that you care for him?" (Psalm 8:3-4). His heart was overwhelmed by God's love and in response he longed to be pleasing to Him. His walk, not without significant stumblings, was marked with a passion for God, who blessed him with the wonderful title "a man after my own heart."

When we fill our minds with thoughts of God's incredible love and power at work on our behalf, praise and joy start to flow. Then, as the Spirit stirs up in us a deep gratitude and passion for God, the natural outcome is a willing surrender of our whole being to Him. Instead of fighting and resisting what God is trying to do in our lives, yielding our will becomes not only possible but the deep desire of our heart. From this surrender of mind, heart, and will spiritual growth comes—that's God's promise.

I'm Living ... Because Christ Lives in Me

What can we expect once we have surrendered our whole being to God? In writing about spiritual growth, John Ortberg, author of *The Life You've Always Wanted*, gives us a picture of what God longs to do in our lives as we live in awareness of Christ in us. He says,

> The goal of such growth is to live as if Jesus held unhindered sway over our bodies.... We are called by God to live as our uniquely created selves, with our temperament, our gene pool, our history.... To grow spiritually means to live increasingly as Jesus would in our unique place—to perceive what Jesus would perceive if he looked through our eyes, to think what he would think, to feel what he would feel, and to do what he would do?[4]

Having Christ live through us doesn't mean good-bye to individuality. We're not put on a spiritual conveyer belt that automatically pummels, pats, and prods us into a preconceived mold.

Think about yourself, your gifts, your personality, and your heart desires. Did God make you with an outgoing, vibrant (okay, loud) temperament, and then say, "To be really spiritual you need to be just like Marcia "super-saint"—all hushed tones dropping like dew from your gentle, calm demeanor?" Not at all. Did He give you a heart for children and then expect you to stride across a platform instructing five hundred women each week like your church's high-profile leader? Of course not. He made you unique and that is what He wants you to be—yourself—with His Spirit living in you and flowing out to bless others.

Discovering what God had in mind when He said He was committed to making us like His Son begs the question: *If Jesus lived through me today, in my unique life situation, what would He do?*

What would you say? A rather mundane but truthful answer for me, right now, is that Jesus would keep on writing. Two hours from now He would prepare dinner for my husband and me. Four hours from now I believe Jesus would welcome our care group into our home and get everyone a cold drink.

Is it enough to simply *do* what Jesus would do? We all know there's a huge difference between doing things with a cheerful spirit and mumbling under our breath at everyone around us while we go through the motions of service. So, to respond as Jesus would, I also need a Christlike attitude. As a writer, that means having an attitude of dependence and asking God what He wants me to write rather than going off on pet peeves or projects. As a wife, I want to feel toward Jim what Jesus would feel when Jim comes home tired and hungry after long hours at the hospital. In my role as hostess of our care group, I want to act as Jesus would, to notice the needs of individuals and reach out to them.

Do I always respond as Jesus would when Jim walks in the door an hour late and the casserole is shriveled up or the salad wilted? I'm still in process, so what do you think? Do I always notice and respond sensitively to the concerns of our care group? No—sometimes I'm preoccupied with my own life, not theirs. So do I need to grow more like Jesus Christ in the unique circumstances of my life? Undoubtedly. Seen in this light, our unique life-circumstances become a constant dynamic opportunity for drawing on the Holy Spirit's power within us to produce spiritual growth.

To live "as if Jesus held unhindered sway over our bodies" is possible even if we have backgrounds that haunt us and certain predispositions and temperaments that we don't like. No matter what handicaps any of us have, we can seek to live our lives as Jesus would, in the unique package that includes who we are and what our personal circumstances happen to be.

Let's ask ourselves, "How would Jesus think about the situation I'm facing at work? What does He see fueling my attitude toward my mother? How would He respond to the needs in my child's school? What actions would He take today if He were in my shoes?"

As you reflect on your own circumstances, how would you answer the question:

If Jesus lived His life through me today, in my unique life-situation, what would He do differently?

As a wife:

As a single woman:

As a working woman:

As a mother:

As a church attender:

In other roles/responsibilities:

In preparing His disciples for His physical departure, Jesus told them He would send His Spirit to live in them forever (John 14:16-17). Because of this promise, we know His power is available every day to us in every situation we face.

In talking to friends about how the Holy Spirit works in our lives to make us more like the Lord, various experiences emerged.

Sally: "The other evening I was hot and feeling irritable. John had just come home and I felt grouchy about fixing dinner. My day hadn't gone well so I felt like taking it out on him. Just then I remembered that I didn't have to act like this. I knew it wasn't the way Jesus would handle a bad day. So right then, I stopped and asked the Holy Spirit to help me release my irritable spirit and give me a joyful one instead—and my black mood lifted."

Hilary: "The Spirit helped me in a battle of wills with my husband. Tom made it clear he disapproved of something I felt free to do and I felt very angry with him for wanting me to stop. As I was praying about it, the words, 'Do you love Me? Will you do this for me?' kept coming.

"I do love the Lord and told Him so, but I rebelled at submitting to Tom's preferences on this matter. Before too long, the Holy Spirit helped me see that *this was a matter of surrendering my wishes to Christ, rather than a question of who should have their way.* By yielding to what I felt God was asking of me, the strain in our relationship was replaced by peace between us. Now I'm praying Tom will begin relinquishing his will to God also, not to please me, but to please the Lord."

Jane: "One of the ways the Holy Spirit has helped me over and over is to give me courage to go through doors He opens. I'm not naturally very self-assured, so whenever I feel overwhelmed, I cry for help, and He reminds me He's with me and will enable me to do what's required. What happens is amazing. I find myself filled with peace and even confidence. In fact, I end up saying, 'Here I am, God. You accomplish whatever is Your will'—and He usually does more than I ever hoped for."

Remember the little Chinese boy I told you about at the beginning of this chapter? He tried so hard to imitate my husband. Of course he never could. He didn't have the power to be anything like him. In our own strength we cannot be more like the Lord. We don't have the power to see what He sees, to think or feel or act as He would. But now that we are adopted into God's family and indwelt by His powerful Spirit, becoming more like Him is possible. Jesus wants to live His life through you at your office, in your home, when visiting your in-laws, or simply driving on the freeway. When you let His Word dwell in your mind and heart and allow Him to have His way in your life, you will experience what you long for—to be more like Jesus.

In any quest to grow spiritually strong, the subject of "spiritual disciplines" comes up. Whenever I read about these ways to draw closer to God, I feel drawn to practice them but, at the same time, overwhelmed with a feeling of hopelessness. I know I don't have whatever it takes to fast for forty days or sit in a garden silently contemplating heavenly scenes. What I do know without a doubt, however, is that I need help in my desire to be changed and that's where the "D" word comes in. Are you ready to keep on learning how to grow in spite of your feelings, flaws, or failures? If so, let's face, head on, the part self-discipline plays. Who knows? You might even be glad you did.

Reflections—for Thought and Discussion

1. Brainstorm on what you think it means to be like Jesus. What do the following verses tell you about Christ's character: Matthew 11:29; Galatians 5:22-23; Philippians 2:3-8?

2. How has the Holy Spirit encouraged, taught, convicted, or enabled you to be more like Jesus? Be specific.

3. Briefly recall the circumstances of your spiritual birth. What did you understand at the time? What have you learned since about what occurred when you became a child of God?

4. What practical difference can the truth that you are "in Christ" make in your life?

5. As a woman living in a world of rapidly changing values, how does being called a "saint"—one who belongs to God—challenge you?

6. What encouraging thoughts or lessons did you find in the section "You're Empowered by the Holy Spirit"? How can you apply one of these this week?

Memory Verse

"His divine power has given us everything we need for life and godliness through our knowledge of him" (2 Peter 1:3).

Notes

1 Hannah Hurnard, *Hind's Feet on High Places* (Wheaton, Ill.: Tyndale House, 1988).

2 Willard Erickson, *Christian Theology* (Grand Rapids, Mich.: Baker Book House, 1983), 952.

3 John Stott, *The Cross of Christ* (Leicester, England: InterVarsity Press, 1986), 148.

4 John Ortberg, *The Life You've Always Wanted* (Grand Rapids, Mich.: Zondervan, 1997), 17.

THREE

Do I Have to Discipline Myself?

PLEASE DON'T CREAK, I PLEADED SILENTLY WITH THE BED. Sliding out from between the warm sheets, I padded quietly to the bedroom door and down the hallway to the kitchen. Breathing a sigh of relief that Malaika, age five, and Elliot, age two, hadn't heard me, I reached for my Bible.

My pleasure was short-lived. Two excited little voices shouting, "Mommy, Mommy," grew louder and louder. Bursting into the kitchen, they clamored for breakfast and attention.

"Lord, it's hopeless," I groaned, as once again my efforts to have time to study and pray were sabotaged. "The early mornings just don't work. Besides, I'm so tired I can barely drag myself out of bed. I'll try spending time with You when they have their afternoon naps."

Getting Malaika and Elliot to synchronize their naptime was a challenge. By the time it finally happened, the thought of spending time focused on God had lost its appeal. All I wanted was a little peace to read a magazine or a book. And so the months went by.

Still, I really *did* want to draw closer to God, to shine with joy, to scatter words of divine wisdom on all those in my path.

I genuinely longed to be like those other mothers I observed who seemed to be able to control their children with little more than an indulgent smile or an occasional raised eyebrow. They never seemed to raise their voices, lose their tempers, or grab for their little angel's nearest limb and hold on until motherly control was reestablished. At the end of many frustrating days when my flaws refused to remain hidden, I would cry out, "Lord, please help me!"

But nothing happened. I didn't change—God didn't seem to be paying any attention.

In the midst of being stuck in deep spiritual mud and going nowhere, I heard about a seminar on discipleship to be held at our church. Hoping I'd discover some simply wonderful formula that would deliver me from myself, I eagerly signed up.

Before the seminar began, I glanced around the fluorescent-lit basement room with its bare floors and plain walls. Bible verses printed in austere black ink on a white background were the only decoration. One of them caught my eye. It was a statement King David made thousands of years ago, declaring he would not sacrifice a burnt offering to the Lord that cost him nothing.

I couldn't take my eyes off it. I felt as if the Holy Spirit were burning the words into my soul. "Poppy," came His inner voice, "the reason you aren't growing is that you're not willing to sacrifice your sleep or anything else in order to spend time with Me. You say you want to be changed, but until you're willing to do what costs you, you'll never see what I can do in your life."

Driving home a few hours later, I still couldn't get that verse out of my mind. "You're right, Lord," I confessed. "Even when You do make time available, I put other interests ahead of You. I had sort of hoped You'd wave a magic wand and change me, but I'm beginning to see that's not the way You work. Lord, I want to make a commitment to You. From today onward I will stop making excuses. I will get up and spend time with You even if Malaika and Elliot are awake."

Now, it would be a bald lie if I said that someone as unregimented as I am by nature has never missed a daily time with the Lord since. I have—because doing the same thing day after day is still a struggle for me. I can't even eat the same breakfast every day— unlike my husband, Jim, who can eat instant oatmeal for years in a row before he needs a change. Discipline and regimentation are in his bones. (I'm convinced his brain was programmed to respond to routine by spending his growing-up years milking cows twice a day and driving tractors up and down endless rows of corn on his father's farm.)

Regimentation and discipline are tough for those of us who are made of different stuff. My commitment to the Lord didn't transform me into a compulsive disciple who studied, memorized, prayed, and witnessed unfailingly. But it did mark the beginning of a new direction in my life.

Bit by bit I began, on most days, to plan specific times to get into the Word and pray. When I did, I found the Holy Spirit had many things to talk to me about. In fact, I invariably found myself convicted, encouraged, or challenged—or all three at once. God began a major overhaul in those difficult years of adjusting to marriage, motherhood, and other personal challenges—but it meant learning the value of discipline.

Do I Have to Discipline Myself?

Discipline, not one of my favorite words, conjures up thoughts of forcing myself to do something I don't want to do. I balk at exercising every morning, flossing my teeth every night, and saying no to chocolate-mocha cheesecake whenever I visit my favorite café. Discipline demands that I deprive myself of something appealing and instead push myself to do the opposite— generally something unpleasant, undesirable, and unrewarding. No wonder it's a battle for many of us.

When you're not a perfectionist, a high-achiever, or on an ego-trip to prove how holy you are, it's easy to ask, "Why should I discipline myself?" And that's a good question. Why should we give up precious sleep, time to read a magazine, or the chance to catch the late show on television in order to read the Bible and pray? Why take time from anything we enjoy doing to grow in our relationship with Jesus?

Our instinctive reaction to imposing discipline on ourselves might well be to reject the idea, but perhaps we need to question and probe our assumptions. God uses various means to bring about change in our lives. Frequently He uses people we clash with to sandpaper our rough edges smooth. At other times, tough circumstances cause us to grow closer to Him. But another method He uses is what Christians have long called spiritual disciplines.

Traditionally the term "spiritual disciplines" covers various activities that enhance our awareness of God—these include silence, solitude, fasting, and giving. In the next chapter we will focus on five in particular: prayer, obedience, intake of the Word, examination, and relinquishment. Put together as an acrostic, they spell the word P.O.W.E.R. If we practice them, that's what they bring into our lives.

Imagine spiritual disciplines as key pieces of equipment in a local health club where various machines exercise different parts of your body. Some require more effort than others. The same is true with spiritual disciplines.

Now, for those of us who immediately back away from any list of "things I've got to do to be spiritual," let's stop and gently ask ourselves some questions we might rather avoid. Could there be benefits to disciplining ourselves? What compelling reasons exist for us to cultivate spiritual disciplines? What motivation is strong enough to overcome our tendency to do only what we feel like doing at the moment?

Let's see what answers we can find to these three questions.

What Benefits Are There to Discipline?

Benefit No. 1: Daily Power

When Jesus said, "Come to me, all you who are weary and burdened, and I will give you rest" (Matthew 11:28), He was offering to give us all that we need to live each day as His children.

This can include the ability to trust God with a problem instead of worrying yourself into an ulcer, the inward strength to keep on working in a negative atmosphere, or a growing boldness to tell others about your faith in Christ.

"Many of the women in my office were hard to like," said Jean, a single administrative assistant in her thirties. "Their language was crude and they talked about their sex lives nonstop. As a Christian I found it a real challenge to care about them. The only way I survived my two years in that job was by praying every day about my relationship with them, asking God for His power to show a genuine interest in their lives."

Like Jean, we find ourselves experiencing sticky situations with other people from time to time. Perhaps your life is marked by strife between you and your husband, a family member, or someone you work with. If so, ask yourself, "What qualities do I need personally for this situation to be resolved in a positive way?" (Check those that apply):

peacemaker attitude

wisdom

self-control

love

other qualities:

Maybe you're juggling taking care of an aging relative, your home, and other commitments, or coping with small children while your husband travels all week. Think of your current situation. What qualities do you need now so that others will see Christ living in you? Write them down:

Jesus tells us where our source of inner power can be found. He said, "You will receive power when the Holy Spirit comes on you" (Acts 1:8). The Holy Spirit lives in each believer. All the power you and I need each day is available to us according to that promise. How can you experience this?

• *Believe* God can create in you what you don't have in your own strength. Faith in God's power to work in you is essential, because without faith it's impossible to please Him (Hebrews 11:6). God is still the Creator, therefore He can bring forth in you those qualities you need.

• *Thank* God each day that His Spirit lives in you and will supply what you need. You have access, through prayer, to the Holy Spirit's power. When you ask Him for what you need, He'll provide it. God promises, "Live by the Spirit, and you will not gratify the desires of the sinful nature" (Galatians 5:16).

• *Trust* God to provide what you need because He has already declared that we are "more than conquerors through him who loved us" (Romans 8:37). Take hold of what He has promised and confidently act in the strength He supplies. Daily power can be your experience when you look at your situation with faith and walk in the light of what God says. Try this: When you pray, lift your empty hands heavenward and simply ask the Lord to fill them with what you need in your life right now. Then meditate on trust.

Benefit No. 2: Daily Input

By choosing to read the Bible each day, we put ourselves in the place of hearing what God wants to say to us *today*. Daily dependence on and awareness of God's constant provision were two of the lessons Jehovah intended the Israelites learn as He fed them with manna for forty years (Exodus 16:1-30).

Some of the Israelites, however, got greedy, lazy, or just plain ornery. They decided, against God's orders, to collect enough for two or three days and then take it easy for a while. Perhaps the women were super-efficient homemakers who liked to make triple batches of everything. In any case, when they woke up the next morning they knew something was wrong. An awful smell filled their tents, and when they uncovered their leftover manna, the sight was ghastly. It heaved with maggots. Aren't you thankful for refrigerators?

Gathering fresh food is still God's intention for us, only now it's spiritual nourishment we need for each new day. To help us see how important this is, let's take a little memory test.

Try to remember something God said to you a few years ago regarding a situation in your life. Write it down. (If you're over forty, I understand if nothing comes to mind.)

What do you recall from last year?

What about yesterday?

Are you chewing on old experiences with God and hoping to get strength for the fresh challenges you face today? Yesterday's wisdom can help, but God also wants to give us fresh input for new circumstances.

Our lives are in constant flux because nothing stays the same. Our children go through new stages of development, our jobs demand new skills, somebody asks us to take on a new responsibility, we face a health problem, our parents become frail. The "manna" we received two years ago, even two days ago, does provide needed wisdom, but God has fresh supplies for what we will face today.

Teresa's life was full with three teenage sons to carpool to school and drop off at various extracurricular activities most days of the week. Her husband, Joe, worked long hours and relied on her to shoulder most of the family needs. Then one day Joe was diagnosed with cancer of the stomach.

"Seeing Joe suffer," she confided, "was more than I could bear. I begged God to give me the strength to be calm and strong for all the family. At other times, when I felt weak and wept with fear of the future, God comforted and reassured me as I told Him how frightened I was about raising the boys by myself." Joe lived three years after his initial diagnosis. What Teresa needed from the Lord changed daily as she moved from being a home-based wife and mom to supporting Joe through all his tests and treatments, to helping their sons deal with Dad's coming death, to becoming a widow in her forties and entering the marketplace to earn a living without Joe.

When we settle for an occasional weekly or monthly snack in the Word, we condemn ourselves to spiritual anorexia and its resultant weakness. Fresh bread is available every day, if we're hungry enough to eat it.

Why practice spiritual disciplines? For two reasons. First, because they bring us before God so He can change us, and second, because unless we do, we'll find ourselves weak when an unexpected situation demands inner strength; blind when God wants us to see what He is doing right in front of us; or tripping and falling where we could have stood as witnesses to His presence in us.

Benefit No. 3: Daily Intimacy

How quickly do you grow spiritually cold? Oh, you can pray in a pinch when your friend looks at you over lunch and says, "Why don't you ask the blessing?" And you can come up with some holy-sounding words or even a Scripture if someone calls you with a problem. But does your hunger for God dry up without fresh input, the way mine does? I can lose my sense of joy and excitement for God so fast it frightens me. How about you? Daily intimacy is like a high-potency vitamin pill, enabling us to:

Grow in awareness of His presence: One of the greatest blessings God offers us is the daily awareness of His presence. Realizing Jesus is with us can calm us down in a stressful situation or pep us up when we're feeling discouraged. But experiencing the positive effects of knowing He's with us happens only when we remind ourselves of this every day, even many times during the day. We might be headed for a scary interview, get rear-ended on the freeway, or receive news that puts our stomach in knots. We might also get promoted or win the "Employee of the Year" trophy. Either way, spending some time in God's presence, praising Him and reflecting on who He is helps us to remember, *God, You love me, I am precious in Your eyes. You are all-powerful, and with Your Holy Spirit who is in me, I'm ready for whatever today throws at me.*

Grow in concern for others: Acting more like Christ and letting His character show in our outward behavior is another result of daily intimacy. A Denver police spokesman, commenting on the beating death of a taxi-driver while spectators watched, expressed horror. "Witnesses saw him being beaten and dragged by his feet but no one telephoned us," she said.[1] We live in an increasingly callous world where violence is becoming commonplace. But even though we need to be wise about personal involvement in many situations, we must not allow ourselves to grow indifferent to people's needs.

If we want to portray more deeply the concern of Christ for others, we need to ask ourselves if we feel and act with compassion when we see people in need—whether on the street or at work. Is our first impulse to get involved and give support to a hurting person at church? Do we stop in the middle of our busy schedule of picking up the kids at school and rushing them to another activity to listen and help? Which is seen more in us—the character of our world or the character of our Lord? Daily intimacy with God through His Word acts like a meat tenderizer. It keeps our hearts from being toughened by the world around us.

Grow in Christian character: Daily intimacy also gives the Spirit opportunity to teach and empower us to live as Christians.

Something lying on the road caught Susie's eye as she was on her daily jog. Looking closely, she realized the "thing" was a wallet. "I picked it up," she said, "and inside found $350, but no name or address. I took the wallet home and wondered what to do. After searching through it again I found the address of a nearby apartment block where the owner lived. He had put the wallet on top of his car, then had forgotten to retrieve it when he drove away."

How did Susie resist the temptation to keep what she found? "I knew keeping the money wouldn't be right in the Lord's eyes," she said. "He gave me the power to ignore all the reasons that popped into my mind for pocketing the money."

God reveals He is at work in us as our character changes, as He answers prayer, *and* as He uses us to touch the lives of others. By seeking His power each day we open ourselves to experiencing His reality in fresh and new ways.

Why cultivate the spiritual disciplines? Because the daily benefits God wants us to lay hold of help us grow spiritually strong and useful to Him. But there are other compelling reasons for doing so.

You're Training Yourself to Be More Like Christ

"Do you know how the Singapore Everest team trained for their expedition?" my husband asked from behind the newspaper. "They climbed up sixty floors of a skyscraper carrying backpacks filled with sand, came down by elevator, and repeated it five times. Their trainer made them do this every other day."

I can't imagine climbing six floors with or without a backpack, much less sixty, or doing it more than once. These team members were dead serious about achieving their goal to conquer Everest.

What about us? How serious are we in our goal to grow spiritually strong? Serious enough to plan our lives around what draws us closer to God, to become more like Christ?

Paul urged Timothy: "Train yourself to be godly" (1 Timothy 4:7). In writing this he taught Timothy something you and I have already discovered. Godliness, the quality of reflecting God's character, doesn't descend from some celestial cloud, and transformation doesn't come via a lightning bolt from heaven. Godliness is the result of asking God to make us alert to Him and then cooperating with what He wants to do in us and in our world. If we want to experience a more alive walk as Christians, spiritual disciplines can't be ignored.

Training ourselves to be godly sounds like a tall order, though. Just what does this involve? Are we supposed to spend all our spare time beseeching God in prayer, digging into the Greek and Hebrew meanings of various theological words, or fasting till we're dizzy and cross-eyed? No. Let's throw out the notion that training is just another word for intense misery-inducing activities.

The concept of "train yourself" carries the meaning of "to exercise or discipline yourself." We all know what that means— if we want to achieve a particular goal we have to put in the necessary time and effort. Some things have to go and other things have to be incorporated into our lives.

Training, not simply trying, is necessary to achieve many goals in life. I tried to ski—once. Not understanding why the ski instructor warned us about turning our backs to the slope, I struggled to my feet after a fall only to find myself sliding backward down the mountain. In response to my frantic cries for help, the instructor and all the other beginners in my group shouted, "Fall down, fall down," which I did—to gales of laughter. Trying my best wasn't enough. I needed serious training.

And trying our best isn't how we find spiritual success. To grow strong, we have to be willing to let Christ become our trainer through regular practice of the spiritual disciplines. When we do, our ability to respond to life as Jesus wants us to becomes more and more likely. But a second compelling reason for discipline exists: it strengthens and displays our priorities.

You're Demonstrating Your Priorities

Remember my cries to God to change me? My fervent longings to have more control over my frustrations and temper? Why didn't I see any transformation at that time? Because what I said I wanted was miles apart from the choices I made. Priorities are only wishful thinking until we put them into practice.

Here's a question you might not want to answer—but answer it anyway. What optional activities take away time you could use to develop your relationship with God? Write them down.

If you're serious about spiritual growth, how could you rearrange your priorities?

You and I might shrink from the thought of cutting something out of our lives in order to spend time with our Trainer, but our part in growing spiritually strong is to discipline ourselves. In contrast to our often negative view of discipline, Richard Foster, author of *Celebration of Discipline*, emphasizes that discipline is the door to liberation and to joy, setting us free from the slavery of ingrained habits and putting us in a place where God can work in our lives.[2]

George Mueller, who took care of thousands of orphans in England, was known as a man of great faith. After addressing a crowd, a young man approached him for help. "Mr. Mueller," he began, "would you please pray that God would get me out of bed in the mornings so that I can pray and experience Him as you have?"

"Young man," responded the elderly Mr. Mueller, "I certainly will pray for you. And I will guarantee that if you get one leg out of bed in the morning, God will get the other one out."

The young man who approached Mr. Mueller apparently hoped prayer alone would supernaturally lift him up from his bed and deposit him on his knees. It doesn't happen like that.

That's why we pray for God's help. He is the one who gives us the longing to know Him and experience His presence, but we must respond by exercising discipline over our bodies, moods, and desires.

Discipline demonstrates we mean business with God, that we want Christ as our trainer. It's the evidence of His claim on our lives. To find out what part discipline plays in your life, ask yourself one more tough question: What role does discipline play in my relationship with God? A lot, some, or a little?

Explain:

We've considered three benefits of cultivating spiritual disciplines: daily power, daily input, and daily intimacy. We've also recognized that change doesn't happen unless we consistently train ourselves, seeking the Spirit's direction in establishing our priorities and the use of our time. This requires discipline.

Let's deal with one more question that undergirds all we've covered so far. Where do we find the motivation to change our lives so growth can happen?

You Were Bought With a Price

According to a recent study, rearing a child born in the United States in 1997 until the age of twenty, will cost almost $150,000. A middle-class child can be expected to eat up to $55,000 worth of food and use over $22,000 worth of clothing. Parents are warned they need to put away more than $319 every month from the time their child is born to have enough money to cover their expenses.[3]

Knowing what it will cost to raise children might well make prospective parents stop and think, but knowing the cost of our salvation didn't make God change His plans. The apostle Peter, speaking of the cost involved, said, "For you know that it was not with perishable things such as silver or gold that you were redeemed from the empty way of life handed down to you from your forefathers, but with the precious blood of Christ, a lamb without blemish or defect" (1 Peter 1:18-19).

Why would God love us enough to give His only Son to die on the Cross, bearing the condemnation we deserved? Certainly He didn't see anything wonderful in any human being, because we've all been infected with the sin virus. The answer lies in His nature. The God who is love is also holy.

Christ died for our sins that He might bring us to God. "Our sins were the obstacle preventing us from receiving the gift He wanted to give us. So they had to be removed before it could be bestowed.[4]

How has your life been changed because of Christ's death for you? Where would you be if He didn't indwell you—providing strength to say no to temptation, flooding you with assurance that you belong to the God of the universe, and reminding you of His eternal presence?

Left to myself, without Christ's presence in my life, I wonder how many times I would have been married and divorced, what scars I might have inflicted on my children, and how many friends I might have wounded. Can you grasp what God has done, not only in removing our guilt and judgment but in saving us from the worst in ourselves?

We have been bought with the precious blood of Christ, a price beyond our ability to understand. This breathtaking truth tells us what it cost God to bring us into a relationship with himself. In Christ, God reconciled us to himself. Isn't this a strong enough motivation to overcome our tendency to do only what we feel like doing at the moment? If we're serious about growing let's discipline ourselves, taking time from other pursuits to get to know this God and learn to delight ourselves in Him.

Spiritual disciplines take the same diligence involved in any kind of training. But the payoff is not just for this life only but for eternity. P.O.W.E.R. to grow spiritually strong and become what we long to be is available. Let's see how to find it.

Reflections—for Thought and Discussion

1. What are your feelings about self-discipline? Would you call yourself a disciplined person? Why or why not?

2. Give some benefits you've experienced from practicing self-discipline as a Christian, a single or married woman, mother, family member, employee.

3. What insights on areas of discipline do you find in the following: Mark 1:35; Proverbs 13:4; Romans 12:1; 1 Timothy 4:7-8; 1 Timothy 6:10-11? How do these verses challenge you?

4. What increases your awareness of God's presence? (Listening to certain music, reading Christian biographies or devotionals, talking to God throughout the day?) Is there some little habit you could begin today that would heighten your sense of His reality and love?

5. How does being aware of God make a *practical* difference in your life—when driving, at home, shopping, around others? Be specific.

6. God is the One who changes us, but we must draw close to Him for this to occur. In light of this, what do you think it means to "train yourself to be godly"? How does this encourage you in your desire for spiritual growth?

Memory Verse

"It is God who works in you to will and to act according to His good purpose" (Philippians 2:13).

Notes:

1 From an article in *Straits Times*, Singapore (March 1998).

2 Richard Foster, *Celebration of Discipline* (San Francisco: HarperCollins Publishers, 1988), revised edition, 1-11.

3 From an article in *Straits Times*, Singapore (March 1998).

4 John Stott, *The Cross of Christ* (Leicester, England: InterVarsity Press, 1986), 64.

FOUR

Where Do I Find the P.O.W.E.R. to Grow?

"LOOK AND FEEL BETTER NOW!" SCREAMED AN
ADVERTISEMENT in the local newspaper for the Grand Opening
of a new health club. "Forty percent off," it promised—off
membership, that is, not body weight. And to convince all of us
wavering, somewhat flabby couch potatoes that we couldn't
possibly pass up this wonderful opportunity, a buxom blonde
smiled invitingly from the page. "Even you," her smile seemed to
whisper, "could look like *me*, if you'd only join up and use our
equipment." I called right away.

"This machine works your biceps," chirped the skinny little half-
girl, half-woman personal trainer. *If you don't watch out,* I thought,
*that spandex rubber band outfit you've poured yourself into is
going to cause you problems.* Oblivious to my inner commentary
she continued, "And this machine does wonderful things for your
triceps."

After half an hour of being told how my triceps, biceps, and
various other " 'ceps" could be physically transformed from flab to
fab by just coming in for one hour, three times a week, I paid my
money. *I'm going to look like you,* I smugly taunted the blonde in
the advertisement.

Unfortunately, my fantasies never materialized. On my first visit, I
diligently pounded the treadmill until the blood in my head made
the lights seem to be blinking on and off, then I tottered over to the
weight-training equipment. Trying to figure out which machine to
sit on and which to lie down on was quite confusing—especially if
no one else was using an identical model. After valiantly pulling
every bar attached to each machine, I attempted the free weights.

Not knowing what size dumbbells I could lift, I tested them out much the same way as I'd pick up grapefruit at the supermarket. Too bad I started with weights that were just a little too heavy.

I didn't mean to drop them dangerously close to yet another skinny woman working out beside me. They just fell out of my hands. Even if I did nearly break her foot, I didn't think that was any excuse for her ugly response to my profuse apologies. *I don't think you're quite up to this yet,* I consoled myself as I slunk away. *You'd better go home and rest. It'll be safer for everyone that way.*

Shortly after my disastrous debut at the health club, circumstances conspired to finish off my fantasies for good. I pulled the rotator cuff muscle in my shoulder—not on the equipment—but at a retreat where I was speaking. The worship leader urged everyone to learn to sign the song we were singing. As the speaker, I could hardly refuse, so I flapped my arms around as instructed. I'd no more than started when a sharp pain shot through my shoulder. That spelled the end of my plans to look like the blond siren in the advertisement. Now, instead of prancing into the health club three times a week, I had no choice but to lie passively under the pain-producing, massaging fingers of a physical therapist.

In spite of my own failure to be a health club success story, club equipment can develop strength in our bodies. But even the most highly rated equipment can't guarantee our success if it isn't used. In addition to machines, we must draw on something within ourselves if we're going to see change—a good supply of both desire and discipline.

Experiencing P.O.W.E.R. to grow spiritually strong challenges us in the same way. Internal issues have to be settled before we proceed to the practical. So let me ask you this: Do you want to grow and develop a love relationship with God? Can you accept the fact that it will take a degree of discipline to begin with, until desire for Him and delight in His working in your life begin to motivate you?

To encourage yourself as you begin this spiritual P.O.W.E.R. program, remember He is drawing you to himself and wants to lead you into a fuller experience of God-centered living. Jesus promised you'd be blessed, not made miserable, when you hunger and thirst for God. What He says is true, so believe it: you're going to be overjoyed at the *new you* that comes from a more vibrant relationship with God. How can this happen? By saying yes to God's invitation to draw close through *prayer, obedience, reading the Word, examination,* and *relinquishment.*

P.O.W.E.R. to Grow: Prayer—Talking With God

"Poppy, I have something I want to show you," said my father, taking a large envelope from a drawer in his desk and handing it to me. "I sent for this information a few months ago and I want to know what you think of it."

Sitting in my parents' living room in England, we were both aware that I'd be leaving the next day to fly back to Oregon. My emergency trip had been filled with the heartache of my mother's untimely death, her funeral, and the sorting through of her things with my two sisters.

Drawing the papers out of the envelope, I gasped. There was a gospel of John, a letter explaining how to become a Christian, and an invitation to send for follow-up material. Why had my father, a seventy-year-old atheist who never had time for God and less for church attendance sent for this material? "Dad," I said, barely able to contain my shock and joy, "Where did you get this? I have been praying for years that you would feel stirred up to ask questions about God and why we are here on earth and what happens after we die."

"That's just how I've been feeling, Poppy," he replied. "Stirred up. So when I saw an advertisement in the Sunday paper offering information about becoming a Christian, I sent for it."

Still in shock, I explained to my father as simply as I could that God exists, He cares about us, and that although I was on one continent and he on another, God could hear and answer prayer. We didn't talk much more that night, and the next day I had to leave. Ten days later a letter arrived from him. "Poppy," he wrote, "I have prayed the prayer to ask Jesus to forgive my sins every day since you left. I've gone into town to buy a Bible and I'm writing down all the questions I have so you can help me when I come to visit." Not only did God transform my father from an atheist into a believer, He directed him to a loving church and a home Bible study group, which he enjoyed for several years.

Have you ever asked yourself, "Why pray? Does it make any difference?" A friend has a plaque in her kitchen that says, "When you stop praying, the 'coincidences' stop happening." It's true. Unless you pray, you'll never know if God answers.

What are your thoughts about prayer? Is it an occasional call for help or something vital to your life? Can you recall any answers to prayer? How about two? Or maybe five or more? Think about your own experience of prayer and record how you really feel about it:

Because we desire to grow spiritually strong, let's deal with some questions about prayer that we might have wondered about but hesitated to ask. First, what is prayer, anyway? Second, why should we pray? And third, how can we be effective in prayer?

What Is Prayer, Anyway?

Ask a dozen people what prayer is and you'll get answers anywhere from "It's talking to God" to "It's asking for whatever you want" to "It's a mystery, I don't have a clue." At its simplest, prayer is talking with God. We bring ourselves with all our hang-ups and longings into His presence, knowing He welcomes us.

Prayer is an expression of dependence. Like the cry of a trusting child looking up to a loving father, we are saying, "I need You." In contrast, to not pray is an expression of independence, as if saying to God, "I can handle this situation with my own resources. I will figure out an answer." When we do this, we refuse the powerful help of God and limit our experience of His reality in our lives.

Of course, there are broader dimensions to prayer—intercession for others so God's power will be released in their lives, praying against the schemes of the Evil One (Ephesians 6:18-20), and seeking a deeper understanding of His love and power at work in us (Ephesians 1:17-19). In essence, prayer is communicating with God to build a close relationship with Him. But prayer isn't a monologue; He speaks to us also through His Word and with the inner voice of the Holy Spirit.

Why Should We Pray?

Amazing as it is, God wants us, His children, to talk to Him, just as we want our children to talk to us. No matter what mood we're in or what situation we're dealing with, He says, "Pray." Prayer is God's chosen way to accomplish His purposes on earth. This is how He releases His power in your life and, through your prayers, into the lives of others.

Because prayer is God's way of releasing His power on earth, Jesus taught His disciples both by example and precept that prayer is vital. John Piper, in his book *Let the Nations Be Glad*, describes prayer as a "walkie-talkie."[1] He envisions Christians as God's army on earth, waging war against a powerful spiritual enemy and needing help from our Commanding Officer—which comes through instant communication with God.

Sometimes our battle with the Enemy is waged in our own hearts and minds, causing us to cry to God for strength to fight back; at other times we're called to fight on behalf of those wrestling against attacks of fear, despair, or great sorrow. We're also to wage war, through our prayers and witness, against the god of this age, who "has blinded the minds of unbelievers" (2 Corinthians 4:4).

Fresh supplies of ammunition, battle plans for victory, and renewed determination to keep fighting are essential if we're to remain standing in these spiritual wars. All of these supplies come when we use our divine "walkie-talkie."

Why should we pray? Because God is worthy of our praise and thanks. He delights in our fellowship. He loves us, is interested in all that happens in our lives, and wants to answer our requests according to what is best for us. Through prayer God releases all the resources we need to live for Him and to accomplish His purposes.

How Can We Be Effective in Prayer?

The best model available to us is Jesus himself, so let's see what we can learn from Him. Both Luke and Matthew record how the Lord prayed at every step of His ministry. Look at the variety of situations they mention: He prayed during His baptism; before choosing His twelve disciples; when the five thousand wanted to make Him king; when the disciples were sleeping in Gethsemane; when He was on the cross.

Through prayer—talking with His Father about every part of His life on earth—Jesus found guidance, strength, comfort, and renewal of vision and purpose. All these inner benefits can be ours as we learn to love God and share every detail of our lives with Him.

Even in His darkest hour of struggle at Gethsemane, Jesus modeled for us four key elements of effective prayer: "My Father," Jesus cried out, "if it is possible, may this cup be taken from me. Yet not as I will, but as you will" (Matthew 26:39). In this one prayer, Jesus taught us to be...

• *Specific.* Jesus didn't pray in generalizations, nor should we. If you ask God to bless you, your family, and all the missionaries around the world, you won't know whether He answered or not. Ask yourself, "What is it I am asking God to do?" Better yet, ask Him what *He* wants *you* to pray for, and begin listening for what comes to mind. Then pray specifically.

• *Transparent.* Jesus didn't wear masks. He didn't hide his true feelings. Nor should we. God knows all our thoughts; we can never fool Him with false words. Be honest with God; nothing will shock Him. It's part of the privilege of talking to the One who loves us deeply.

• *Persistent.* Jesus prayed three times in the Garden. He also taught His disciples that they should "always pray and not give up" (Luke 18:1). Many answers to prayer come after a period of waiting, but in our world of "it should have been done yesterday," we assume God is saying no when His answer might well be "not yet." Learning to persist in prayer is essential to seeing God's answers.

• *Submissive.* For prayer to be effective, our requests must be consistent with God's will. Praying for a Porsche, to win the lottery, or for your boss to be sacked so you can have her job, is not prayer that honors God. Not only should our requests fit in with God's purposes, we ourselves need to be right with Him. That means asking God to help us to want His will rather than our own. To accept His way of answering our request rather than demanding it to be our way. To wait for His timing even if we can't make sense of it.

Jesus said, "Not my will, but Thine be done." Getting to the place where we can sincerely say this to God is essential if we want answers to our prayers. If this is a struggle for you, but part of you indeed wants to grow closer to the Lord, begin by asking Him for the desire to want His will. The closer you draw to God in your struggles, the more He will draw near to you, to change your heart and your outlook (James 4:7-8).

To help you establish prayer as part of your daily lifestyle, here are some additional helps:

1. *Set a consistent time for prayer.* Yes, I know being consistent is often part of our problem, but remember, we're learning to become more disciplined. You can get out of bed half an hour earlier, or find a private spot during your lunch break, or set an earlier time than normal to go to your bedroom and talk to God. Ask God what would work best for you—perhaps right now the best is a few quick minutes as you nurse your baby or fix dinner. Accept that, watching for other moments that open up through the day. Tell God you want to be with Him but need His help to find the best time, then follow through.

2. *Study the prayers of Scripture.* Personalize them, putting in your name or that of someone you're praying for. If your mind goes blank when you start to pray, or you want to pray like God's people recorded in Scripture, open your Bible to a prayer in the Old or New Testament or pray through the Psalms. Read the verses phrase by phrase to God and then expand with personal praise and requests that come to mind.

3. *Keep a prayer notebook.* Buying ones with the days of the week and types of prayer already printed are helpful as thought starters, but it's easy to use any kind of notebook and tailor it to your needs. Take a page per day and on each page list specific requests for family, friends, missionaries, organizations, countries, heart desires, or anything else that you feel called to pray for or about. When you receive letters or photos from those you pray for, tuck them in the page on which they're listed and you'll have a fresh reminder of their needs.

4. *Write out your prayers.* If your heart is moved to respond to a Scripture you've read or to circumstances you're facing, write God a letter. Pour out your feelings as the psalmists did. Express your deepest longings or hidden fears.

5. *Find someone to pray with.* Try asking two other Christian friends to form a triplet and pray for friends or co-workers who don't know the Lord. Look for one other person and ask if she will pray about being your prayer partner. Share your needs with each other every week. Whatever form it takes, when we have others to pray with us on a regular basis, we grow in prayer.

None of the spiritual disciplines that provide P.O.W.E.R. to grow strong can work alone. *Obedience* is essential if we want our prayers answered. *The Word* is needed to show us how God wants us to live. *Examination* opens the way for the Spirit to point out what needs correcting, and *Relinquishment* is the response when our hearts are wanting God's way more than our own.

Now that we've seen the value of prayer, let's zero in on the issue of obedience. What's so important about doing what God says?

P.O.W.E.R. to Grow: Obedience—Saying "Yes" to God

Think about this story. Debbie, a young mom, had two small children, three-year-old Timmy and six-month-old Melissa. While Debbie talked on the phone to her girlfriend, she sorted out a kitchen drawer and kept an eye on the children. But as time went by, she got more and more engrossed in her phone conversation and paid less and less attention to Timmy, who was playing with his baby sister.

After talking for almost an hour on the phone, Debbie hung up and turned around to get Melissa. Shocked, she realized both children had vanished. Rushing down the hallway to Timmy's bedroom, she found him playing with his truck and Melissa gurgling happily on her back.

"Timmy," said Debbie in a voice that spelled trouble, "Mommy told you to never pick up the baby. You could hurt Melissa. You're not big enough to carry her. You disobeyed Mommy."

"But Mommy," cried Timmy, tears beginning to trickle down his face, "I didn't pick her up, I rolled her down here."

Does Timmy remind you of yourself at times? God has given us specific instructions, but, like Timmy who found a way around his mother's instructions, somehow we rationalize away what we know to be right and proceed to do what we want. It's easy to read, "Forgive one another," and to think, *I will when she (or he) has apologized.* Or to know we're to pray for those in authority over us yet to tell ourselves, *When the group I agree with is in power, then I'll pray.*

When Paul wrote to the Christians at Philippi, he specifically complimented them on their obedience to God (Philippians 2:12). What was it that earned his praise? Paul was struck by the fact that they didn't only obey God when he, Paul, was with them. They also obeyed God when he was absent. Why did they do this? Because obedience to God wasn't something they felt pressured into. It was their heart's desire. They longed to please God first, to do what made God happy.

Is that how you feel? Or does your desire to please God ebb and flow depending on your circumstances or moods? Is it conditional on who's present? Reflect on these questions for a moment, then freely write down your honest reactions:

Obedience extends beyond how we act in public when others are watching. It also applies to what goes on in our homes— how we treat our spouses, handle our children, or speak to relatives or friends, but it doesn't stop here. No part of our life is to be roped off from God and posted "Keep out. Private property." Not even the privacy of our thoughts. Listen to Paul's statement about this part of us that we tend to consider as nobody's business but our own. He said, "Take captive every thought to make it obedient to Christ" (2 Corinthians 10:5).

"I used to spend a lot of time daydreaming about John, my old flame," confessed Hope. "My marriage wasn't very happy so having imaginary conversations with him made me feel better. In my mind, John always called me by his special name for me and we would talk and talk. Of course, it was all fantasy, but it felt so good. Then one day, as I was imagining our having this intimate, loving conversation, I felt the Lord saying very distinctly, 'You are married to someone else, and this does not belong in your life. As my child, even your thoughts should be pleasing to me.' I realized then that if I am to walk in obedience, even my mind needs to be surrendered to Him."

Has God shown you a few ugly bugs that you are allowing to grow in the warm privacy of your mind? Our thought life seems to be a perfect sanctuary for harboring grudges, sexual fantasies, or ways to get what we want. It's also the place our enemy, Satan, gains a foothold from which he can harass and tempt us to thumb our noses at God and do our own thing. Obeying what God asks of us goes beyond acting like a nice, sweet Christian woman in front of others, even our families. Obedience goes to the core of who we are and what goes on in our minds where no one can see—no one but God, that is.

When Jesus calls us to follow Him, why does He place such a tremendously high value on our obedience? Let's look at three reasons:

1. *Obedience proves we love Him.* How would you feel about someone who told you they loved you, yet did all sorts of things that hurt you or damaged your reputation? *Fine kind of friend she is,* you'd probably think. Jesus declared, "If anyone loves me, he will obey my teaching" (John 14:23). Words are easy to say. Any of us can spout wonderful words of love to God, but the

genuineness of our declarations is demonstrated by action. Has He shown you something you do or think that needs to be changed? Let obedience prove your love.

2. *Obedience proves we trust Him.* Doing what God says can be tough. When Joshua was told by God to get the Israelites ready to cross the River Jordan, obedience was the proof of trust (Joshua 1:1-2). When God asks you to do something that is very difficult—to restore a broken friendship, to forgive a father or husband for betraying you, to wish the best for someone who got the promotion you wanted—your obedience proves you trust God. Although our feelings might be screaming, "I can't do this," moving forward in obedience, like Joshua, says, "God, I know You love me and mean this for my best. I trust You, and I believe that You will help me to act as your child, regardless of circumstances."

3. *Obedience proves He is Lord.* We live in a world that says, "Don't let anyone tell you what to do," but as Christians we're called to willingly let Someone Else call the shots in our lives. When we say yes to Jesus and obey what He says, even if it's costly, we're declaring to those around us that following Him is more important than putting our self-interest or our "rights" first. To do this means Jesus is the Lord, or Master, of our lives. Because the power to grow depends on making Jesus the Lord of our lives, we'll explore this subject in more detail in the next chapter.

If you want to become what you're not—yet—be prepared to feed your soul with the ultimate soul food—God's Word. Without it, you can't be a strong and healthy Christian. It's like eating your greens, protein, vitamins, and everything else necessary for vigorous life, all in one dish. Add reading the Word to prayer and obedience and you'll feel spiritual muscles developing where previously you've been wimpy and weak.

P.O.W.E.R. to Grow: The Word—Listening to God

Did you know that blind people can ski? How do they do it? They are paired with sighted skiers who teach them on the flats how to turn. After mastering this beginning skill, they progress to gentle slopes where their instructor shouts, "Left!" or "Right!" By listening carefully and doing exactly what they are told, they ski the course without any mishaps.

We can no more see where we are going in life than those blind skiers on the slopes. Like them, we also need to listen attentively to our Instructor and follow what He says. Through reading and studying the Word, God directs us along the right paths and helps us avoid unforeseen obstacles.

The writer of Hebrews says, "We must pay more careful attention, therefore, to what we have heard, so that we do not drift away" (Hebrews 2:1). Paying attention to the Word is essential for growing spiritually strong. Let's see how this works by delving into Psalm 119 and pulling out some of the benefits that come to those who read and heed what God says.

Benefits From Reading God's Word—Psalm 119

* *Purity* (vv. 9, 133). The battle for purity is no longer limited to young men or women. It's an arena we all find ourselves in. After becoming Christians, most of us discover fairly quickly what major, moral commands we're to follow. We tend to think of the Ten Commandments, add "Love your neighbor," and assume that as long as we follow these we're okay. But in a world that has an amazing ability to make what was once clearly black and white turn to various shades of gray, we need to look again at what God's Word tells us.

When you wonder what to think about issues discussed over the water fountain at work or at the beauty shop, get out your Bible.

That will halt any mental or moral drift. Find out what God has to say and anchor your beliefs firmly on His truth.

* *Counsel* (vv. 24, 98, 104). Where do you turn for advice? "Dear Abby," a horoscope, various friends, or your Bible? New Age gurus, the Psychic Network, and a multitude of other counselors with strange backgrounds and philosophies all crowd around, claiming to have answers for your life. Who you listen to can have far-reaching consequences.

If you need counsel, God promises wisdom, knowledge, and understanding—when you seek out what He has to say, that is. Buy yourself a concordance, which lists every reference of a particular word found in the Bible—this will be an invaluable tool for finding out what God has to say on a given subject. Try reading a chapter a day (or even less) from the book of Proverbs and see how much sound counsel is available in just this one book. Then keep reading in other parts of the Bible because it is saturated with sound principles for dealing with the issues in your life.

* *Freedom* (vv. 45, 130). Do you want freedom from guilt? Freedom from plaguing mental put-downs? Freedom from self-pity? You'll find that walking in freedom from whatever binds you comes as you seek out God's teachings about what He has done for you, who you are, and your worth in His eyes. It's all in His Word. As you read, the Holy Spirit will affirm in your heart, "I am God's child—loved, forgiven, set free to live for Him." Retrain your mind with the Word of Truth, and you'll be on your way to liberating freedom from past bondages.

* *Hope* (v. 147). Do you sometimes wake up feeling discouraged or a bit blue? What do you do about it? Drag around and wish you could go back to bed? Better to stop and let your mind be lifted upward by God, declaring like the psalmist, "I have put my hope in your Word."

We can put our hope in a lot of other places: our jobs, our friends, our investments, our children. All of them will fail us at one time or another. What does God's Word promise? We have Someone who is there for us every day of our lives, who has plans to bless us and will ultimately take us to be with himself forever. Read the Word and discover countless reasons for hope. Let them sink in and buoy you up—out from whatever pit you find yourself in. Satan is the god of discouragement, but Scripture abundantly demonstrates that our God is a God of encouragement and hope.

Try reading through Psalm 119 for yourself, highlighting all the other benefits listed that come from reading the Word. Think about them, see how they apply to what is happening in your life, then act on what you've discovered.

Before we leave this psalm, let's turn the spotlight on what it teaches about treasuring the Word in our hearts. Unless I do something more than merely scan words on a page before rushing off for the day, I find it hard to remember much at all. How about you? Do you want to profit from being in the Word? Then absorb the psalmist's attitude and actions and watch yourself flourish.

* *Expect a blessing* (vv. 1-2). Before opening your Bible, pray that God will open your heart to His words. Reading the Word isn't an academic exercise to increase your head knowledge. God speaks to you from these ancient pages, drawing you to himself, and bringing you a blessing of joy, comfort, courage, or whatever you need at the time. Look for a promise to claim, a command to obey, a truth to believe, a name of God to fill your heart with praise— expect a blessing.

* *Seek God with your heart* (vv. 10-11). Jesus said that seed sown on good ground will always bear fruit (Mark 4:20). What's required for a spiritual harvest, a reaping of power, and change in our lives? A soft, receptive heart open to whatever God wants to

say and plant deep within us. Your response to God determines the fruit.

* *Apply your mind* (vv. 13-16). The Bible will have no effect on your life if you can't remember what you've read. These words are meant to be our sword, a fighting weapon by which we defeat the Enemy's lies and enticements. Jesus showed us how effective this can be when He used Scripture He had memorized to defeat Satan in the wilderness.

Even if we're convinced that memorizing a verse a week is beyond us because we're too disorganized, distracted, forgetful, or lazy—most of us could do it if we considered it important enough. After all, we can remember phone numbers, addresses, and birth dates—at least most of the time.

Why not do what the psalmist recommends and hide God's Word in your heart?

Don't stop with memorizing a verse. Meditate on it. Chew over each word, asking yourself what it means and what the verse as a whole is saying to you in your circumstances. Get the nutrients out of what you're memorizing—then you won't suffer like an undernourished infant from a failure to thrive. The Word is meant to feed you, make you grow strong, and provide you with an internal, dynamic power source.

Begin today with one verse. Write it out, take it on your walk, stick it on your dashboard, or prop it up around your house where you'll see it. Repeat this every week. However you do it, get the Word stored in your mind and heart.

Reading the Bible on a regular basis opens our eyes to how God wants us to handle events in our lives—and, all too often, we discover His ways are very different from ours. For example, don't most of us grumble and complain, at least some of the time? Guess what—as Christians we're told to stop it. A whiner isn't the kind of advertisement God wants. What happens when we read these kinds of commands in the Bible? The Holy Spirit is speaking, telling us it's time for a little spiritual examination.

P.O.W.E.R. to Grow: Examination—Seeing What God Sees

After the end of World War II, many people were desperate to escape from Eastern Europe into the newly liberated Germany. In order to do this, however, they had to run the terrifying gauntlet called no-man's land.

Crossing this area patrolled by dogs trained to track down humans, and watched over by Soviet soldiers with machine guns mounted on high towers, meant their prospects of survival were minimal. The most frightening aspect of all was the searchlights. Sweeping back and forth over this forbidding stretch of land, countless people were caught in the blinding light. Many froze like terrified animals, waiting for the shooting to begin, while others tried to run.

In contrast, during that same war, my mother spent several months in London while waiting to join my father, who was assigned to a Royal Air Force base in the north of England. Finding herself there during the horrifying blitz of London, when German bombers flew over the city every night, she was required along with every other able-bodied person to take her turn on watch. Standing on the roof of a building, her job was to watch the searchlights as they scanned the skies, trying to spot the enemy planes. On seeing a bomber caught in the searchlight's beam, she was responsible to sound the alarm so people could rush for safety to the air raid shelters. The day after she left London to join my father, the building she was assigned to was demolished by a bomb.

Did you know that one of the Holy Spirit's roles in our lives is to act like a searchlight? But His intention isn't to flood us with fear like those Eastern Europeans who cowered in terror. Rather, the Spirit's purpose is like those searchlights in London, to warn us of impending danger. By powerfully scanning our motives, ambitions, and values, He shows us where the Enemy is sneaking into our lives to cause spiritual damage.

The psalmist understood this and said, "Search me, O God, and ... test my thoughts. Point out anything you find in me that makes you sad" (Psalm 139:23-24 TLB). He called upon God's Spirit to give him a spiritual checkup: was there something in his thinking that displeased God? Perhaps lust, envy, or hatred? Criticism of others? Pettiness? Was there something in his way of living contrary to God's will? He dared to know so he could get right with God.

Spiritual examination is something we invite the Spirit of God to do. It can be at a particular time, such as before taking Communion. It can also be a request to God before you read the Word or at the close of each day. What's important is that we open ourselves up to the searchlight of the Spirit—but be wise in this. Don't confuse God's protecting light with the harmful glare of the Enemy.

The Spirit will convict you of a specific sin or hindrance that is keeping you from living fully for God. Satan, on the other hand, will try to bathe you in a self-loathing that whispers, "You're worthless, useless, and unwanted by God." His goal is to crush your spirit with guilt and condemnation.

Be aware that when you become morbid, depressed, or defeated, this is not God speaking to you. In fact, the Spirit's conviction always comes with the warm promise of forgiveness and loving awareness that God's grace never fails to be continuously available to us.

"When I heard that Angela had received special praise from our supervisor," Susan confessed, "I have to admit I was envious. In fact, it rankled me more than I thought it would.

"The next day I realized I was still nursing some sour feelings about her success, so I decided I had to get right with the Lord. Much as I didn't like to admit it, I confessed to God that I was jealous of her. I asked His forgiveness and began to pray for His continued blessing on her life. By doing this I enlisted God's help to stop Satan from creating a rift between us. God wiped away my ugly, petty attitude and gave me peace."

The loving work of God's Spirit shows us where we're allowing the Enemy into our lives, as Susan found out. This particular spiritual discipline, *examination*, plays a vital part in our spiritual growth because of its power to keep us walking close to the Lord. Make it your aim to cultivate David's heart attitude, inviting God to "point out anything you find in me that makes you sad."

Once we've said this to God, though, we need to be prepared for what He might show us. If we mean business with Him, there will inevitably be times when He calls us to relinquishment. Let's see how this works out in our lives, producing spiritual strength and making us more like Christ.

P.O.W.E.R. to Grow: Relinquishment—Giving Up What Grieves God

"Elliot," I said to my thirteen-year-old son, "look at those pictures on the front page. I feel so sorry for those starving children in Ethiopia." Elliot said nothing. He was engrossed in the sports page of our local newspaper. I tried again to get his attention. "Elliot, maybe you could one day be a doctor as well as a pilot and go and work in refugee camps and help these desperate people." No response.

I was about to try a third time to gently "guide" him toward my plans for his future path, when the Lord got my attention. Softly, I felt Him say, "Poppy, let Elliot be who I want him to be." I knew God was telling me to give up my plans, my wishes, and my

73

expectations. Pushing Elliot along the path I had in mind for him not only wouldn't work, it wasn't what God wanted and planned.

What kinds of things does the Spirit shine His searchlight on? Here are some areas that affect most of us:

Expectations. These involve our children and regularly extend to our spouses. What expectations do you have of your

husband? Face frankly what frustrates you about him and you'll know. How about your church leaders or people you work with? What about expectations of yourself? When we can't control another person or get what we want from them, it's easy to peevishly think, *Why can't you be different?*

If we're also unrealistic with the expectations we have for ourselves, we set ourselves up for bouts of anger and depression. Look at your expectations. Is the Spirit telling you to release these so you can recognize and appreciate what He has provided for you?

The flesh. Another area the Spirit might shine His searchlight on is the flesh: laziness, self-indulgence, self-pity, easily hurt feelings, or bitterness. We love to nurse the flesh, catering to the enemy within us. Rooting out what the Spirit spotlights often means battling our wills because "the sinful nature desires what is contrary to the Spirit" (Galatians 5:17). But the Spirit won't let us alone. His work is to make us holy from the inside out.

Pride. Have you been around people who scorn Christians as intellectually inferior or as a bunch of hypocrites? How hard did you find it to speak up? Paul said he gloried in the Cross of Christ. Do pride and the need to look good in other people's eyes keep us from identifying ourselves as Christians? Maybe our pride rears its ugly head in some other way. Wherever the Spirit uncovers pride's presence, He's calling us to relinquishment, to let go freely of whatever blocks our fellowship with God.

Guilt. The apostle Paul could have let guilt, like a chain around his ankle, shackle him to the past. What keeps you anchored to your past, unable to move forward in living for Christ? When the Holy Spirit shines His light on something that fills you with shame and guilt, or that you make excuses for continuing, confess it. Be freed forever from its crippling effects.

Desires that become demands. Left unfulfilled, even normal desires for a home, child, fulfilling job, or good health, can over time trigger sinful responses of bitterness and anger. Has God chosen not to answer your particular requests through the years?

Are your dreams drying up? Is there hidden resentment against God in your heart? Here again the Spirit goes about His mysterious work, exposing what is within, calling us to relinquishment.

Gethsemane was the place where Jesus said, "Not my will, but Thine be done." In His loving purposes to make us strong and useful to Him, He will call us from time to time to our own private Gethsemane. Usually we struggle, wrestle, and argue with God. But when we emerge from this place of relinquishment, we will, in time, turn and call it the place of blessing.

Now that you've discovered where the P.O.W.E.R. to grow comes from, let's think about what matters most. With all the different directions you could take in life, with all the calls to "put yourself first," how can you, as a woman wanting to grow spiritually strong, sort out your priorities? Let's see what answers we can find.

Reflections—for Thought and Discussion

1. How do you explain prayer to someone? What would you say to encourage them to pray? Share any new or helpful thoughts on prayer found in this chapter.

2. Why is obeying God sometimes the last thing we want to do? Can you recall a time when you did obey and experience God's blessing? What happened?

3. Review the references from Psalm 119, then think about the time you spend reading and reflecting on the Word. What lessons for yourself do you find from the psalmist's attitude toward the Scriptures?

4. Try to identify any hindrances to reading the Word you personally battle with—for example, time, concentration, organization, desire.... What has helped you?

5. What did you learn from the section on "Examination"? How do you discern between the Holy Spirit's conviction and Satan's condemnation?

6. Do you sense God speaking to you about "Relinquishment"?

Can you identify what He is putting His finger on? How will your response help or hinder His work in you?

Memory Verse

"Let the word of Christ dwell in you richly as you teach and admonish one another with all wisdom" (Colossians 3:16).

Notes:

1 John Piper, *Let the Nations Be Glad* (Grand Rapids, Mich.: Baker Books, 1993), 41.

FIVE

What Matters Most?

"DID YOU HEAR WHAT HAPPENED TO ANN?" MY FRIEND Kathy asked. "Her house burned down yesterday and she lost everything. No one was hurt, fortunately, but all of Ann's books, photo albums, personal mementos, her computer, and organ— everything is gone."

My heart grieved for Ann. Her tragedy also made me wonder. *What if my home were on fire?* I mused. *What would I try to save if I had a chance?* I know I'd want to save my books but I couldn't carry all of them out. No, the two things I'd make a desperate effort to save would be as many photo albums as possible and all my teaching notes.

How about you? What items are so important to you that you'd make every effort to rescue them from a burning home? Obviously people and pets would come first, but then what would you race to save—dishes that were passed down through your family, jewelry, a Persian rug? What comes to mind will give you a good idea of what matters most to you.

Because of our busy lives, we frequently put off identifying what matters most to us. Whether it's what we would save from a burning house or what we want our lives to amount to, our tendency is to put off answering the question until a critical moment arrives—and then it's often too late. As Christians, however, the question *"What matters most?"* has both earthly and eternal significance. Unless we think now about what's really important, we can end up frittering our lives away or investing them in pursuits that amount to nothing from God's point of view. This can happen to any of us.

"My aunt just celebrated her seventy-fifth birthday," said Gloria. "As we talked about her life, one of her comments struck me to the heart. She said, 'I wish I had lived more for the Lord and less for myself.' She felt she'd wasted opportunities to make a difference in people's lives." Gloria hesitated, then added, "Made me wonder ..."

Getting to the end of our lives and looking back without major regrets *can* happen. We can't go back and undo our previous choices, but we can make wiser decisions today and in the future with God's help. Out of all the daily and long-term choices swirling around us, what matters most is what pleases God the most—lovingly and joyfully *giving our lives to Him*, then *living our lives for Him.*

A World of Choices

As women you and I live in a time of unprecedented change and opportunity. We face choices never before available to us. Not all of these freedoms please God, but let's review some of them— honestly and openly.

We can choose whether or not we want to marry. The days of being handed from father to husband against our wishes is are long gone. In fact, we can choose whether we even want a husband or not. If we have one, we can also legally trade him in for a new model. Furthermore, once we discover that we're no longer financially dependent on a man to survive, there's nothing to stop us from opting for the single life.

We can choose whether or not to have children. Married, divorced, or single, lesbian or heterosexual, technology can help us have a child or abort it. Adopting a child is also more feasible than at any other time in our history.

We can choose to have a career. No longer the domain of men and a few women, the female sex has joined the marketplace in historic numbers. CEO's, lawyers, physicians, college professors, and engineers who are women abound in every city, and the sound of glass ceilings being shattered no longer causes much of a stir.

We can choose to pursue anything we're drawn to. From Generation X'ers to Busters, Boomers, and grandmothers, women are free to choose where they will invest their energies. Do you want to pursue higher education, run for political office, or establish your own business? In today's world, little besides finances can stop you from trying. The number of choices available today can plunge us into confusion or challenge us to explore new paths. With so many avenues open to us and conflicting views about what we women should choose to do at different seasons of life, we can be thankful that God promises to give us wisdom when we ask for it.

We can choose what kind of person we want to become. None of us is set in concrete. We can choose to be the kind of person we want to be. God's help, always available, never runs out. The kind of person we are and the kind of person we want to be is a matter of choice. We can stay stuck in a sourpuss mind-set, raising our eyebrows and being critical of others, or we can be women who reach out to others, forgive slights, and control our tongues.

"My parents' relationship was rather stormy," confided Martha. "Mom was very strong-willed and outspoken. If she didn't agree with my father or want to do what he suggested, she'd lose her temper and go into a verbal tirade. This was my model for a husband-wife relationship." Half-smiling, she continued, "When I got married, as you can imagine, I reacted like my mom when Mike asserted himself or said something I didn't like.

"After a few years of this kind of behavior, God got hold of me and began opening my eyes to see how I was damaging my marriage. Mike reacted just like my dad—he withdrew. Soon a big wall grew between us. I was mad because he wouldn't talk to me, and he felt he didn't dare say anything because I would only criticize him.

"One day I heard someone say, 'Ask God to show you how your husband sees you.' I did—and what I saw was so bad, all I could do was tell God how much I hated who I had become and ask Him to change me. That process has taken a long time, but I'm definitely not who I once was."

Martha chose to change because she wanted to please God. Now when she looks back over her life, instead of being plagued with regrets about how she treated Mike, she can feel at peace. "By deciding to stop doing the things I did to make our marriage miserable," said Martha, "we not only have a more fulfilling relationship, I also have the joy of knowing I'm pleasing God. Plus, when Mike saw the change in how I treated him, he changed his reactions to me."

If you and I want to grow spiritually strong, we too have to think through what matters most to us. Can you say, without hesitation, that you want to please God in every dimension of life? If you can, you've discovered the key to a life of meaning and fulfillment. God won't waste your abilities or sit you on a shelf when your aim is to please Him. He's got plans to develop all the potential He's put in you, and to make your life count for eternity.

*Giving your life to Go*d and *living for God* are two conscious decisions we're called to make after we've said yes to Christ. Just as salvation affects our lives both now and for eternity, so do these key decisions. In fact, they are so powerful they determine how useful, joyful, and fruitful our lives as Christians will be. For this reason, let's see what *giving your life to God* and *living for God* really mean.

Give Your Life to God

An old story is told about a chicken and a pig. As they approached church one Sunday morning, they noticed that the sermon topic on the sign board read, "What can we do to help the poor?" Being a quick thinker, the chicken immediately said, "Well, we can serve them bacon and eggs."

The pig thought for a moment and replied, "There is only one thing wrong with feeding bacon and eggs to the poor. For you it requires only a contribution, but for me it requires total commitment."

Commitment—the Path to Effective Living

Giving our lives to God involves far more than making a contribution to a worthy cause via a check, or even offering to teach the three-year-olds' Sunday school class every week, noble as that may be. The pig was right on target—total commitment to God means giving all we have and are to Him—finances, possessions, ambitions, loves, and longings. This means saying, "Here's my life, Lord. It belongs to You. Show me how to live each day with Your purposes as my priorities."

Jesus never watered down the fact that there is a cost attached to following Him, but He also promised, "Whoever loses his life for my sake *will find it*" (Matthew 10:39). Whatever term you use for this transaction with God—commitment, dedication, or consecration—this step puts you in the path of blessing and effective living. In essence, you are giving the Holy Spirit free rein to change you and work through you to carry out God's purposes. When you lose your life by giving it to God, you will find out, as Jesus promised, what true life is all about.

Let's focus on the cost involved for a moment. We are told to expect some form of persecution or discrimination; it is an accepted part of being a follower of Christ. For Christians in many parts of the world, however, persecution can be far more than

81

merely being looked down upon or dismissed as intolerant or a little bit fanatical. For them, choosing to live for God can mean prison sentences, being cast out by their families, even death.

When facing any degree of rejection, we're not only privileged to be identified with Jesus who suffered for us, we're also blessed. "Blessed are you when people insult you, persecute you and falsely say all kinds of evil against you *because of me*," said Jesus. "Rejoice and be glad, because great is your reward in heaven" (Matthew 5:11-12).

Because of the Holy Spirit's power in us, instead of licking our wounds and feeling sorry for ourselves when we're treated negatively because of our faith, we can respond like Jesus would— with joy and peace. We'd better be sure, however, that any ill-treatment we experience *is* because of what we do for Christ and not due to our own un-Christlike words or behavior.

When we commit ourselves to God, we're saying to Him, "I believe that giving myself to You, without reserve, is the smartest thing I can do. In fact, it's the only way I can live a truly fulfilled and purposeful life, because You know what's best for me." When we do this, we are acknowledging God's loving ownership of us: "You are the Potter and I am the clay— and I trust You, Lord, to mold me into whatever kind of vessel You can and will use."

Wanted—Living Sacrifices

Paul also talked about the importance of giving our lives back to God when he wrote, "I urge you, brothers [and sisters], in view of God's mercy, to offer your bodies as living sacrifices, holy and pleasing to God—this is your spiritual act of worship" (Romans 12:1). Once we have experienced God's mercy in saving us, He wants to take us to a deeper level with himself. Going beyond our delight in His love for us, He calls us to surrender our bodies, our minds, our souls to Him. It's a little like offering the keys of your car or the access number to your bank account to someone—only this all-powerful Someone won't do anything that isn't for your best. In fact, He declares that He will work all things together for your good.

Even as living sacrifices, however, we're bombarded daily with the temptation to jump off the altar where we offered ourselves to God, take back our submission to His will, and run our own lives. When the cost of going God's way gets too tough, be warned; this can be a powerful attraction. So what holds us steady? Deciding *what matters most*: that as Christians, Jesus Christ is worthy of our devotion, His claim on our lives is not something we take lightly, and no matter how difficult His molding process becomes we want to do what pleases Him.

God longs to accomplish His purposes through each one of us—so He calls us to follow Him. This is exactly what Jesus did when He came to earth. He said, "My food [satisfaction, fulfillment, joy] ... is to do *the will of him* who sent me.... I have brought you glory on earth by completing the work *you* gave me to do. I seek not to please myself but *him* who sent me" (John 4:34; 17:4; 5:30, emphasis mine).

Can you say the same to God? Is your satisfaction found in doing His will? Are you involved in some sort of work for Him? Is your longing to please God rather than yourself, even if it costs you financially or affects your career or social life? Take a few moments to think about these issues—then ask God to help you respond to the following:

Have you ever given your life unreservedly to God—what you have, who you are, where you want your life to go? If not, what is holding you back?

Jesus promised that if you lose your life for His sake, you will find it. Likewise, we're called to offer ourselves as living sacrifices. If you've never taken this step before, will you do it now? Write out your commitment as a prayer, inviting God to work out His loving purposes in your life.

Self-Will—Our Persistent Enemy

Giving ourselves to God isn't a one-time transaction. Satan tempted Jesus in the desert and then left Him, but only for a time. Giving up after one try isn't his style. His goal was to persuade Jesus to forget God's plans and take the easy way out, and he tempts us to do exactly the same thing. "There's no harm in doing that," he whispers. "No one will find out." And if we give his enticements a moment's consideration, down we go.

Don't be fooled. Your commitment to follow God's will rather than your own is going to be tested in many different ways as you move through life. Every time we succumb to the seductive, inner voices of the Enemy or of our flesh and jump off the altar asserting *our* self-will, we're saying, "I am the master of my fate, the one who will decide what's best for me." Fortunately, the Holy Spirit doesn't respond, "You're on your own, babe." Because He's committed to continue to work in us until the end, it isn't too long before He springs into action. For those endowed with a strong streak of self-will (doesn't that include most of us?), sensing an inner conviction of wrong by the Spirit can become a fairly common experience.

After I sensed God leading me out of teaching with Bible Study Fellowship, Peggy, one of my leaders, asked me over lunch, "What will you do now that you've resigned? Have you thought that God might want you to be a retreat or conference speaker?" "Why would I want to do that?" I responded rather strongly. "I doubt that most of the women attending retreats remember anything the speaker said two weeks later, so why would I want to invest hours of studying, praying, and preparing for it? I'm sure some of the women are spiritually hungry, but I think many of them are just out for an all-night slumber party with their girlfriends."

Looking shocked, Peggy said, "Well, I guess if that's your attitude, God won't use you in that kind of ministry."

Driving home after lunch, the Holy Spirit began His work. "Poppy, I thought you had given your life to Me. Since when have you decided what you will or will not do in my kingdom? And have you forgotten that my Word doesn't return to me without accomplishing what I sent it out to do?"

By the time I arrived home, I was thoroughly repentant. Kneeling by my bed, I asked God to forgive me for ever telling Him what I would or would not do with my life. Acknowledging that He—not I—was the Lord of my life, I recommitted myself to serve wherever He wanted. That experience of jumping off the altar and deciding what I'd do with my life—but then quickly getting back on—led to many exciting opportunities to serve the Lord. In fact, it opened up rivers of blessing that I still splash around in.

However, that powerful streak of self-will and self-determination never seems to lie down and die. Oh, it pretends to be dead, but it's really sneaky. Just when you feel most devoted to God and in your deepest secret thoughts even wonder if you have an invisible halo hovering over your head, the attack comes. Self-will jumps out laughing and says, "Ha-ha. You thought the battle was all over didn't you? Well, guess what? I'm still here!"

Several years after telling God I'd do whatever He wanted, I agreed to teach a women's Bible study for a year at a local church. After three months, however, I found myself restless, wanting to take some classes at a local Bible college, and plotting how I could get out of my commitment.

To my delight, Anne, a former missionary, agreed to take over the class starting in January. But when I looked at the college's winter schedule, I realized nothing would work for me. Every class I wanted to take occurred on a day I couldn't attend. I started to feel a little uneasy and wondered, *have I pushed ahead of God and decided my own agenda again?*

Two weeks before the women's Bible study was to begin, I received a phone call. "We're really sorry to tell you this," said the women's ministry director, "but Anne isn't able to take over for you. She has to have emergency surgery—and she'll be out of commission for three months. Can you keep teaching the class?" I would have to have been spiritually deaf not to get God's message. Back I went, and discovered, as is so often the case, that God had hidden blessings stored up—blessings I would have missed if I'd gone my own way.

And Your Prize Is ...

Giving our lives to God not only determines our impact and fulfillment on earth, it also has an eternal dimension. One day we will give an account to God for how we lived as His children. Paul speaks of this when he says, "We make it our goal to please him.... For we must all appear before the judgment seat of Christ, that each one may receive what is due him for the things done while in the body, whether good or bad" (2 Corinthians 5:9-10).

Notice that our appearance before the Lord has nothing to do with our salvation, rather it has to do with how we lived as Christ's followers.

A familiar statement goes, "Only one life, 'twill soon be past. Only what's done for Christ will last." It's also true that only what's done for Christ will be rewarded.

A minister conducting a funeral was told about the deceased: "He never did any harm." The minister confessed he was strongly tempted to respond, "But did he do any good?" Paul urges us, "Be ready to do whatever is good" and "whatever you do, do it all for the glory of God" (Titus 3:1; 1 Corinthians 10:31). That's the criteria by which God looks at our lives.

No doubt when that great day comes all of us hope to hear the Lord say, "Well done, good and faithful servant," rather than "Now tell me, just what happened to you?" To avoid the possibility of the latter statement, we need to do as Paul urged and "make it our goal to please Him." This means choosing to live our lives for God—saying yes to a lifestyle that puts Christ in charge of everything from our time to our treasure.

Live Your Life for God

What characterizes someone who lives for God? Lace-up shoes, a bun, a big frown? A large, black King James Bible tucked under an arm? Thank goodness it's none of these things. This is what living for God looks like: Those who live for God find out what matters to Him and then do all they can to live it out.

But it isn't always that simple.

"I'd appreciate your prayers for a situation I'm in," said Helena. "There's a young boy in our apartment block who is very destructive, and his parents don't want anything to do with him. He's been told by them to stay outside until past ten at night. I found him playing with matches and have heard he's also been cruel to animals. It's obvious he's got a lot of problems. What do I do?"

Here's a second scenario:

"My boss allowed certain rules to be broken and someone was hurt at work," said Jean. "Now he wants us all to lie to the inspectors if we're interviewed individually. If we don't, the others can make life pretty miserable."

Consider a third dilemma:

"I grew up with the assumption that you followed a career path, even if you had young children," said Laura. "Now I have a baby, and I'm having all sorts of struggles about leaving her in daycare. What should I do?"

Living for God often involves complex situations. In today's high-speed, high-pressure world, we need scriptural priorities tattooed on our minds more than ever. Just what matters most in God's eyes? Can we know? And is it possible to live it out? We certainly don't lack guidance from Scripture—we just have to grab hold of it, fixing it in our gray matter and in our hearts. For starters, here are some principles to set you on the path to living for God.

1. *Begin with the end in view.* You'll hear this principle taught by today's savvy time-management experts, but David the psalmist said the same thing to God long ago: "Show me, O Lord, my life's end and the number of my days; let me know how fleeting is my life" (Psalm 39:4). At twenty, the years seem to stretch before us like the interstate highway across Montana—there's no end in sight. Move to mid-life, however, and you wonder what happened to the last few decades. You feel as though you were trapped in one of those bullet trains hurtling through endless miles of scenery—it all went by so fast you can't recall anything in detail.

A healthy awareness that life is fleeting serves as a powerful motivation to be proactive about our lives. Because making changes in ourselves or our circumstances takes energy and focus, simply reacting to whatever comes along has strong appeal. However, taking the path of least resistance won't help us become what we're not. In order to squeeze the most practical help out of this principle, unlock your imagination.

Begin by projecting yourself forward toward the end of your life. Now don't picture yourself as wrinkled and haggard—what you look like then has nothing to do with what we're talking about! On second thought, maybe it does. If we go through life smiling instead of frowning, maybe we'll look pretty good at that point in time. In any case, forget how you might look for right now. Instead, focus on answering the following questions:

* As you picture yourself at eighty or ninety, what kind of person do you hope to be? Do you want to be as you are today? Or do you long to see some changes in yourself? Write down what comes to mind:

* Mull over what you hope will have characterized your life. A friend's great grandmother had the following epitaph: "She was a loving wife and mother, and a friend to all." What would you like to be said about you? Jot down your thoughts:

* Focus now on priorities. Which ones do you hope were so important to you that they guided your life?

* Think of your major relationships in life. What would you like to be true of your attitudes toward those closest to you?

* When you look back, will you feel you invested your life or frittered it away?

By answering these few simple questions, you've taken some important steps toward uncovering what you'd like your life to amount to. No one knows what life will bring, but you can take responsibility for how you respond. Looking at your earthly existence from the end backward spotlights not only what might need changing in your life, it also provides what we all need— powerful motivation! After all, you really don't want to end up an unhappy and wrinkled old lady, do you?

2. *"Seek first his kingdom and his righteousness ... "* (Matthew 6:33). What do you spend much of your time thinking about? How to stretch your money to cover all the bills? How to advance in your career? How to afford some snazzy new clothes?

The command to seek first His kingdom and His righteousness was addressed to people who literally didn't know if they'd have food to eat at the end of the week or enough clothes to keep warm if there was a sudden cold snap. Those were days without walk-in closets, bulging freezers, or well-stocked pantries. Worry today might well be over how to pay for all these items, plus the new deck, and that sparkling four-wheel-drive sports utility vehicle parked out front.

Seeking God's kingdom first by letting His priorities direct the use of our time and money can seem a trifle idealistic in our "produce or be let go" world. Pressure to prove your worth by working ten-plus hours a day is the norm. Stopping to ask, "Is this how God wants me to live?" often doesn't occur until some part of our life comes crashing down.

"I didn't realize how my career had become my idol," said Alison as we talked about putting God first. "At the beginning I just wanted to help the company start up and be successful, but before too long I was putting in crazy hours every day. I told my husband to feed the kids frozen pizza and put them to bed. Then the company went broke. I lost my job, and now God is showing me how skewed my priorities had become. I had no time for my family, and less for Him. I existed for my work."

If we're going to live for God, guided by His priorities, we need to ask ourselves, "What do I exist for? Do I merely tell myself that His kingdom interests are most important in my life? How do I know they are?" What's your response?

3. *"Whatever you do, work ... as working for the Lord"* (Colossians 3:23). When God put Adam in the Garden of Eden, it wasn't to loaf around in the sun nibbling grapes. He was told to work. And so it is for each of us. Our work may vary from keeping house to keeping the books of a major company, but meaningful work is a gift from God. Without anything satisfying to do on a regular basis, most of us would find ourselves slouched in front of the TV wondering, *Is this all there is to life?* When you look back, is that what you want to see?

"Whatever you do, work at it with all your heart, as working for the Lord, not for men.... It is the Lord Christ you are serving," says Paul (Colossians 3:23-24). As you think about looking back on your life, what work would give you a deep sense of satisfaction? Caring for your children? A particular kind of employment? Or serving as a volunteer in a cause that matters to you? What comes to mind?

The kinds of work we do in life may vary, but our ultimate Employer never does. It is the Lord Christ you serve, even if your supervisor, family members, or committee chairperson bears no likeness to Him. Offering every day to our real Employer lends significance to everything we do—from changing diapers to dealing with clients.

In order to look back without regrets on the role work played in our lives, we need to remember some sobering truths. God never intended work to supplant our relationship with Him, to be our sole source of significance, or to become the cause of broken marriages or neglected children. As you think about living for God, what changes might you need to make in your attitude or work habits to please your ultimate Employer?

4. *Live as children of light* (Ephesians 5:8). Paul doesn't leave us to wonder exactly what this means as he goes on to say, "For the fruit of the light consists in all goodness, righteousness and truth ... find out what pleases the Lord" (vv. 9-10). Living to please God challenges us to tell the truth and to do what's right—two qualities that sometimes make us squirm.

As I dressed in the bedroom one Friday morning, Jim called out to me from the bathroom, "What are these black spots on the new carpet?"

Oh no! I thought. The day before I'd been experimenting with some hair dye, trying to hide stray strands of gray appearing around my hairline. But living up to my "Sloppy Poppy" name given lovingly by my parents years before, some of the dye had splattered on the new off-white bathroom carpet. I was caught!

If I tell Jim I dripped hair dye on the carpet, he's not going to be very happy with me. But how can I lie? The temptation to claim innocence was almost overwhelming, until I remembered what day it was. *It's Friday,* I thought in a panic. *There's no way I can lie. I have to go and teach my Bible Study Fellowship class (BSF), and how can I do that if I've just lied through my teeth?* I knew I was trapped. It was tempting to lie to avoid confessing but I couldn't disobey God so blatantly.

"I don't know why you don't just let yourself go gray" was all Jim said after I confessed.

Sometimes I don't want to do what I know is right. One of the flaws I've had for many years is trying to get out of things I don't feel like doing anymore. But God is working. Now, the reason why I don't feel like doing something can vary. I'm tired of the commitment, bored doing the same old thing, feel scared and inadequate, don't want to expend the energy, or there's something far more appealing going on at the same time. Wouldn't you know, I'm married to a man who considers reliability and keeping your word an indication of character strength—and the lack of it, a character weakness. Even though I don't always like what he says, I'm glad God put him in the place of helping me grow in this area.

One summer during the years I taught for BSF, my tendency to evade demanding situations raised its ugly head. *You don't really want to teach for another whole year, do you?* asked my flesh. *It takes so much energy and it limits your time for other things such as shopping. Just imagine all the tennis you could play and the craft malls you could cover. Why, you could even take up gourmet cooking—a sure hit with Jim and the kids.* It was all so appealing and reasonable. Surely everyone would understand, and God would provide someone else—doesn't He always? When I raised the possibility with Jim, his response was swift.

"How can you even think of such a thing?" he asked incredulously. "You gave your word months ago. You can't go back on your commitment now." And that was that. The Holy Spirit had spoken quite decisively through my husband, and I knew it.

How about you? Are you aware of some character flaws that are being worked on or need to be worked on? Ask yourself, "Where am I tempted not to tell the truth or to do the right thing?" Write down what the Holy Spirit pops into your mind.

Don't be discouraged by the flaws you've faced up to. Abraham lied. Sarah was a bit of a shrew. Jacob deceived people. Moses lost his temper. And Miriam was jealous. There's hope for you and me. We will become what we're not as we keep opening ourselves up to the Spirit's work to help us live as children of light.

5. *Redeem the time.* "Can't stop now, gotta run," cries your friend. "Oops, sorry, that's my cell phone, got to answer it," says your buddy. "Really want to catch up. Let's make a date, but it has to be next month," shouts your old school friend as she dashes off. Time presses on. We rush and meet demands. We end up exhausted. What's the answer?

Create margins, declares Richard Swenson, M.D., author of *Margins: Restoring Emotional, Physical, Financial, and Time Reserves to Overloaded Lives.*[1] "It is important that we gain control over our own lives," he says. "When we understand that we are finite and that it is okay to be finite, then we can begin to accept our limits with comfort." Pushing ourselves, our families, or others we work with into overload is detrimental to our health, our relationships, and our walk with God.

Living your life for God means learning to rethink your priorities, making whatever adjustments are called for in each new season of life. "Don't live carelessly, unthinkingly. Make sure you understand what the Master wants," urges Paul (Ephesians 5:15-16 THE MESSAGE).

Molly, a young mom, didn't want to look back with regrets about how she used her time, so she figured out her priorities and determined to stick to them. "I know that at this season of my life, being a full-time mom is God's calling," said Molly. "I'm happy to serve at the kids' school or in the church, within limits. But knowing what's important to me right now, I don't let myself get pressured into saying yes to everything I'm asked to do. Even if someone calls and says, 'Please, please consider taking on the leadership of this committee because, if you don't, the annual "whatever" won't happen,' I can say no without any guilt."

When you've settled on what's really important for you at a particular season of your life, you've got a compass to guide you in your use of time—and you don't have to feel that you're letting people down or that no one will ever speak to you again. Give yourself permission to say no, because what you're really saying is yes to those priorities God has shown you are most important.

Charles Hummel, author of *Tyranny of the Urgent*, says, "We live in constant tension between the urgent and the important.... If the Christian is too busy to stop, take spiritual inventory, and receive his assignments from God, he becomes a slave to the tyranny of the urgent."[2]

Does this sound familiar to you? Is the pace at which you're living one that God has given to you? What else might be driving you to live with overload? Think about the tyranny of the urgent and the need for breathing spaces, margins, in your life. What changes might God be asking you to make so that you live with His priorities?

6. *Build relationships.* Proverbs 14:1 declares, "The wise woman builds her house, but with her own hands the foolish one tears hers

down." The "house" represents all the many relationships that form the fabric of our lives. If we want to be women who look back with satisfaction on our lives, we need to be builders not destroyers—and words are one of our most powerful tools.

You are so ...

How would you complete the sentence if talking to a friend, your husband, or your child? What comes to mind might be telling you something! Your words pack a punch—lifting someone up or flooring them for a long time to come. Proverbs 18:21 rightly points out that "the tongue has the power of life and death." Positive words are like verbal chocolates people relish for a long time. When you share them, you create bonds of caring and forge warm relationships. But words can also rip and shred apart when used carelessly or callously.

A young man went to his village priest one day and confessed that he had gossiped about another person and ruined his reputation. "What can I do to make amends?" he asked.

"Take a feather pillow up to the bell tower," replied the priest, "tear it open and let the feathers fly on the wind. Then go and collect them all."

"But that's impossible," protested the young man.

"Exactly," said the priest. "What you have done can never be fully undone."

Sometimes we hurt others without meaning to. But, at other times, we knowingly use our tongues as weapons to stab, wound, or gossip. Stand back and look at how you speak to those around you. Are you accomplishing what you most desire—or tearing down what is most precious to you? Record your thoughts, perhaps as a prayer to God.

Scripture exhorts each of us to encourage, build up, and comfort one another—activities that require warm and caring words. If you want to look back without regrets, learn to practice tongue control. It's something we can all benefit from.

7. *"Each wife is to honor her husband"* (Ephesians 5:33 THE MESSAGE). A poster in a women's club advertised an upcoming discussion on "What Makes a Happy Marriage?" Beneath was the question: "What do you and your husband have in common?" Some witty woman had scrawled: "We got married on the same day." Hopefully you and your husband have a little more in common than your wedding day. Some couples are like twin peas in a pod—they love to go everywhere together, do chores together, and even choose their clothes together—matching their colors, of course. Then there are those who really do wonder, *Just what do we have in common?* Regardless of the kind of marriage we have, living our lives for God means doing all we can to keep them alive and exciting. Here are some areas in which a little attention can pay big dividends:

Turn up the affection level: Remember, you're not living with a permanent fixture like the fridge or washing machine—he's alive, and so are you. Pat him on the head, stroke his neck, or squeeze him tight. Light a fire under your relationship and get some sparks flying. To settle for living like pieces of furniture under the same roof is asking for it to cave in.

Pour on appreciation: "Thank you for helping me with..." seems like such a small thing to say, but do you do it? On a regular basis? Are you teaching your children to do the same? Think about the qualities you appreciate in your husband and tell him—either face-to-face or via a note or card. Proverbs 16:24 says, "Pleasant words are a honeycomb, sweet to the soul and healing to the bones." They also go a long way toward healing a dry or fractured marriage.

Make yourself as attractive as possible: What kind of a sight are you to behold when you say good-bye in the morning and hello in the evening? Cute, perky, somewhat put together? Or something else? Break some bad habits if need be but make yourself appealing to your husband.

Taking your marriage for granted, as if it could never go down like the *Titanic*, is unwise in today's climate of easy divorce. Think about what makes your husband happy—is it a willingness to curb your spending, or taking care of something he can't get to, or listening to him without interrupting or contradicting what he says? Figure out what creates conflict between you and what brings harmony. Aim for the latter and you'll be on your way to a stronger marriage.

As you reflect on the above, what one action on your part would have the most positive impact on your marriage? Will you put it in writing as a commitment to God, proving your willingness to act on what He's shown you is really important?

Giving our lives to God for His purposes and then *living our lives for God* opens the door to deep and fulfilling spiritual growth. However, as we continue to mature as Christians, we soon discover that what we think about ourselves, others, and God himself powerfully affects our responses to what comes our way.

You might question, "Does it matter what I think?" The answer is, what goes on in our minds—what we think and tell ourselves—can cause us to stumble in our Christian walk or wonderfully spur us on to live for God. Let's explore why.

Reflections—for Thought and Discussion

1. If *your* home were on fire, what would you try to save? Why?

2. Aside from material possessions, what else is most important to you? Try to rank these in order from one to five.

3. What does *giving your life to God* mean to you? How would making this spiritual commitment change you or the way you live?

4. In what areas do you struggle with self-will? How do you deal with it?

5. Reflect on the section *Live Your Life for God*. Look up the biblical reference given for each principle. What application to your life do you find in these verses?

6. List as many reasons as you can for *giving your life to God* and for *living your life for God*. Use this list to identify your priorities. Ask someone to pray for you, lovingly holding you accountable as you begin to make necessary changes.

Memory Verse

"We pray this in order that you may live a life worthy of the Lord and may please him in every way: bearing fruit in every good work, growing in the knowledge of God, being strengthened with all power according to his glorious might" (Colossians 1:10-11a).

Notes:

1 Richard A. Swenson, *Margins: Restoring Emotional, Physical, Financial, and Time Reserves to Overloaded Lives* (Colorado Springs, Colo.: NavPress, 1992), 222-223.

2 Charles Hummel, *Tyranny of the Urgent* (Downers Grove, Ill.: InterVarsity Press, 1967).

SIX

Does It Matter What I Think?

I WAITED ANXIOUSLY FOR JIM TO ANSWER MY CALL FROM England, where I was visiting my father. As the phone rang and rang, I fretted, *Oh, come on, Jim, please be home. I've got to talk to you.* Finally he answered.

"Has Interest magazine arrived and is my article in it?" I asked, after a quick greeting.

I felt crushed and embarrassed. Jim tried to cheer me up but I felt like a failure. After finding out how he and the children were faring by themselves, I hung up the phone. Then I started to berate myself.

Obviously, your first attempt at writing an article was a failure, I chided. *Why did you ever think you could do this? You know you don't have the training or experience to write something worth publishing. Give up the idea of writing; it's clear you can't do it.*

My inner tongue-lashing continued even after I arrived home in Portland, Oregon, a week later. Then one morning I decided to really listen to what I was telling myself.

Immediately, I recognized some tapes stored in my mind from years before. "Poppy, don't push yourself. Give up, it takes too much effort. It's not worth the trouble. Just relax and enjoy yourself," advised my well-meaning mother.

Instead of coming from a home where my sisters and I were challenged to do better, our parents indulgently and kindly urged us to take it easy. Decades later this same message still tempts me to give up when growth demands effort and perseverance.

After recognizing what was happening in my mind, I decided it was time to talk back and tell myself the truth. *You're not a failure just because you tried and failed, I told myself firmly. If you don't try, you'll never find out what the Lord can do in you. Giving up is not the way to grow and become a person God can use.* After talking to myself, I talked to God.

"Lord," I prayed. "You know I did my best, even though it doesn't look like it was good enough. I want to serve You with whatever gifts You've given me. Being realistic, Lord, I know gifts need developing just like any skill, so I'm not going to give up. I'm going to keep on learning and trying. The results are up to You."

A short time later, I stood in the kitchen chatting to a friend. "By the way," Dave said, "I really enjoyed your article in this month's *Interest* magazine."

"What are you talking about?" I asked in shock. "It was supposed to be in last month's issue. Are you sure it was my article?" Dave hadn't made a mistake. When my copy of the magazine arrived, there it was, along with an editorial note saying the article was meant to be in the previous issue but had been held over due to lack of space.

Guard What You Think

Does it matter what we think? Absolutely. What we think and tell ourselves can affect the direction and quality of our lives. Emphasizing this truth, Scripture urges, "Above all else, guard your heart, for it is the wellspring of life" (Proverbs 4:23). Since "heart" and "mind" are often used interchangeably in the Bible— one speaking of our emotions, the other of our thinking—a paraphrase could be, "Watch what you think, for that's where life is determined." Why the warning? Because our mind is of strategic value to God—and to our Enemy. We're told to guard it because it's the control center of our lives.

When I met my husband in Kenya, his job was to look after the medical needs of Peace Corps volunteers. Forget any romantic notions about his living in a simple mud hut in a jungle clearing, swinging from tree to tree clad in a loincloth. Jim lived in a three-bedroom brick bungalow, complete with a servant who ironed his clothes and polished his shoes—tasks my husband to-be assumed I would carry on once we were married. (The ironing, yes. The shoes, no.) In addition to his cook/housekeeper, he also employed a gardener, and a guard to watch the property at night.

Because gangs of thieves broke into homes on the outskirts of Nairobi, the guard was responsible to watch Jim's house and sound the alarm if robbers appeared. On several occasions, however, Jim arrived home around midnight to find the guard snoring in front of the door.

Now, the guard's job was to watch for tricky intruders, be alert to trouble, and sound the alarm if danger threatened. Did he do this? Not at all. He slept through the night and had no idea if robbers were waiting to pounce. In fact, the only alarm he raised during the two years he worked for Jim was one night at about two a.m. when he pounded on the front door shouting, "Simba! Simba!" A lion had decided to stroll through Jim's yard and the guard wasn't about to be eaten in the line of duty.

What about us? Are we asleep, like Jim's guard, and blind to damaging intruders sneaking in through our minds? Do we take seriously our task to guard what influences us, what we think about—as Solomon advised? If our attitude toward life, ourselves, others, and God springs from our mind, we'd better guard what goes into it—because what goes in shapes what comes out.

In view of this, let's ask ourselves some preliminary questions:

Do I question intruding, disturbing thoughts—or give them free entry to do great harm?

Am I careful to shut the door against negative thoughts about others—or do I let them just slip in?

Am I alert to distorted ideas about God—or do they lurk undetected in my mind?

Am I spiritually asleep or awake? Aware or unaware of what's at stake in the battle for my mind?

Speaking out of wisdom learned through his own failure, the apostle Peter writes, "Be self-controlled and alert. Your enemy the devil prowls around like a roaring lion looking for someone to devour. Resist him..." (1 Peter 5:8-9).

How does the devil attack? He has quite a bag of assault weapons, and every one of them works through our minds. Notice his tactics: He deceived Eve's mind in the Garden; he distorted the Word when tempting Jesus in the wilderness. And he constantly looks for ways to discourage Christians through pessimistic thoughts. With an Enemy like this out to devour us, we need to be alert to anything that prevents our growth.

The Mind—Satan's "Gotcha" Place or God's Growing Place?

Our minds are one of God's most fascinating gifts, but they are a little like personal portable nuclear warheads. When programmed properly through input from the Word all is well. But if programmed with all sorts of inaccurate information about ourselves, other people, or God, watch out.

What we tell ourselves puts us either in Satan's "gotcha" place or God's growing place. Think about how this works: if we tell ourselves a situation is hopeless, what happens? Down we spiral into a web of fear and discouragement. Definitely not where God wants us to be. Now, if in the same situation we tell ourselves God is with us and will work on our behalf, what happens? Our faith and confidence spiral upward instead, releasing a sense of peace and power to face whatever comes. In the first case, Satan's got us. But in the second, God has caused us to grow.

What goes on in our minds also causes physical reactions, as I've experienced on many occasions. By indulging my flair for the dramatic, I can easily imagine all sorts of terrible tragedies happening to my children. These thoughts are so realistic that before I know it, tears are rolling down my face and my heart beats faster. It's crazy, but my body reacts and my mood plunges. It's as if what I'm thinking is really happening.

On other occasions, I've had passionate arguments with someone in my imagination. As a result, I'm usually not only steaming mad with them, I find myself more easily irritated with those around me. My personal nuclear warhead is ready to detonate—all because of my thoughts. However, after a deeply personal conversation with someone in my mind, I feel relaxed and soothed—especially if they think I'm wonderful and agree with me on every issue.

Whether we fill our minds with negative facts or pure fantasy, make no mistake: What we think about does affect us—emotionally, spiritually, and physically. So what do we need to do? We must train ourselves to think the truth—about ourselves, other people, and God himself.

Think the Truth—About Yourself

Most of us have mental tapes that start running as soon as we make the slightest error. Listen to yourself. Do you hear some of these statements?

Give up, you can't do it—you're too dumb, too uneducated, you'll always fail.

They don't want you involved—you're ugly, fat, talk too much, and don't fit in.

When God handed out gifts, He skipped you—you can't sing, speak, serve like....

How do you feel when these tapes get stuck and go on and on in your mind? As you've seen, it doesn't take long for me to slump into feeling defeated, embarrassed for trying, and determined to stay well within my comfort zone.

Are we doomed to always tell ourselves the same damaging statements, to believe what was said to us long ago, to be immobilized by thoughts and assumptions we've never questioned? No! But breaking free from the kind of thinking that shuts us off from growth doesn't happen automatically. We need to take some definite steps.

1. *Recognize what influences your self-talk.* Whether negative messages have come from our parents, a teacher, or someone else, they can burn themselves into our minds and become part of our belief about ourselves. We can even be the source of our own distorted thinking.

"I hated school," said Diane, a gifted women's leader in her local church. "I always felt dumb, so I constantly called myself 'Dumb Diane.' Doing this, of course, just kept convincing me all the more that I was dumb. In the end, this thought had such a powerful hold on me that I managed to persuade my parents to let me drop out of school at fifteen."

Sandra's destructive self-talk belittled not only her intellectual abilities but also her looks. "My husband is extremely intelligent," she confided, "and I feel so stupid around him. He also works with many beautiful women, and I feel so ugly. My mother always said I wasn't very bright or good-looking, and now I find myself repeating her comments. As a result, I feel very jealous and insecure around other women. I don't know why Justin married me. I don't have beauty or brains."

Misery-inducing messages gnaw away at our personal and spiritual growth. These messages can range from "I'll never amount to much" all the way to "I'm a failure if I'm not the best, look the best, and have the best." In either case, this inner programming produces emotional anguish. Think about the messages you tell yourself. Which ones pop up unbidden? "I'm always late; I'll never be able to handle money; I'll never be good enough to... ?" Do you ever feel this way? Write down some ingrained beliefs you wrestle with.

What gets fed into our minds lodges, lives, and lurks there—unless we carefully evaluate all input. To break the bondage of lies, start examining what you feed into your mind.

2. *Review and challenge your thinking.* In battling negative programming, it's essential to challenge what we tell ourselves. Our goal is to discover what is true and what is false. Begin to do this by asking and answering these questions.

Why do I think this about myself? Is what I'm telling myself based on truth or assumption? How do I know it is true? What facts support or contradict what I'm believing?

Is what I'm saying to myself biblically true? Answer the question, "Did my heavenly Father say I am useless, incapable, unspiritual, never good enough, etc.?" (Fill in the blank.) It's been said that when the Good Shepherd speaks to His own, He never uses words of despair, hopelessness, frustration, defeat, discouragement, fear, confusion, or failure. Instead, the tender Shepherd offers hope, rest, victory, peace, power, joy, triumph, and love.

What kinds of words do you regularly hear in your self-talk? Do these inner messages reflect the words of the Father of Lies or of your loving heavenly Father?

What are the consequences if I believe this? What we tell ourselves has far-reaching consequences. For example, I could have given up attempting to write. Diane could have refused to let God use her in ministry to others. Sandra could have continued running herself down, pointing out to her husband his mistake in marrying her, and endangering their relationship.

When we believe what isn't true, we cut ourselves off from much that God wants us to experience and accomplish for Him. When your inner messages tell you, "God can't really love me," you forfeit a wonderful sense of security, a spiritual birthright. When you tell yourself, "I'll never change," you're succumbing to the Enemy's tactics. "I can't do that" hides the thrill of discovering your God-given potential—once you fight through those scary feelings. Negative self-talk is costly. Think back, then write down how your self-talk has affected you and the choices you've made through the years.

Why does my mind think negatively? Go for the root of the weed lodged in the corner of your mind. Probe and question what causes your negative self-talk. Remember Elijah? He ran from Jezebel in panic, felt totally useless, and prayed to die. Talk about being overwhelmed by negative thoughts. What caused him to think this way? Sheer exhaustion! Elijah's depression can be traced to the constant stress of fighting a harassing enemy.

When you find yourself thinking negatively, ask yourself, "Is this stemming from stressful circumstances, fears, a need for control, or hormones?" Run a checklist through your mind when you start verbally whipping yourself. Look for the root causes.

3. *Replace negative self-talk with the truth.* When Diane challenged her own "dumb" stereotype, she realized the evidence proved this wasn't true. "After all," she accurately reasoned, "I can analyze information, lead committees, plan programs, and teach what I've studied and learned personally. I might not be well-educated, but I am a capable person."

Assessing her abilities humbly but honestly enabled Diane to shake off some lifelong lies—lies that trapped her in shame and fear of failure. The Word tells us not to think more highly of ourselves than we ought (Romans 12:3). Nor are we to think negatively about who we are and what Christ can do in and through us.

Diane's experience can also help us begin to think truthfully about ourselves. To begin this process,

Ask the Holy Spirit to help you question any automatic, negative assumptions that come to mind.

Make a practice of challenging defeatist and discouraging thoughts.

Replace these thoughts with accurate statements based on facts, not feelings, and with scriptural truth.

"The unfolding of your words gives light," said the psalmist (119:130). And "light" is what's needed in order to guard our minds and fight damaging tapes from the past.

Begin to make a list of biblical truths as you start on the road to transformed thinking about yourself. Memorize them, savor and celebrate their meaning, and soon they'll flash automatically into your mind, battling and defeating your negative self-talk. Here are some to kick off your list with:

> I can do everything through him who gives me strength. (Philippians 4:13)

> God will meet all [my] needs according to his glorious riches in Christ Jesus. (Philippians 4:19)

> God did not give [me] a spirit of timidity, but a spirit of power, of love and of self-discipline. (2 Timothy 1:7)

> For [I am] God's workmanship, created in Christ Jesus to do good works, which God prepared in advance for [me] to do. (Ephesians 2:10)

There is now no condemnation for those who are in Christ Jesus. (Romans 8:1)

It is God who works in [me] to will and to act according to his good purpose. (Philippians 2:13)

4. *Reject the unreal.* Scripture urges us to renew our minds with what is true, real, and upbuilding. When we imagine ourselves failing and being humiliated or fantasize about being in some terrifying situation, we're thinking about what isn't real at all. After all, it hasn't even happened and very likely won't. By indulging our power to imagine, we scare ourselves and walk around filled with all sorts of anxieties, based solely on what we've conjured up in our minds.

In her book *Loving God With All Your Mind,* author Elizabeth George discusses her battle with negative thoughts and their effect on her life. Focusing on the biblical command "Whatever is true ... think on these things," she writes, "Stated in the positive, God is issuing the command, 'Let your mind dwell on what is true or real.' Turning the words around to the negative, the same command would be 'Do not think on things that are not true or real.'

"Here, in Philippians 4:8, God was telling me not to think about anything that wasn't true or real."[1] After this insight, Elizabeth George began asking herself if what she feared or imagined was true or real. If it hadn't happened, except in her imagination, she refused to let herself dwell on it because it wasn't real. By using this Scripture as a weapon against negative thoughts and the feelings they produced, she learned to overcome her struggles with depression and moodiness.

Neil Anderson, author of *The Bondage Breaker*, says, "The center of all spiritual bondage is in the mind."[2] The center of spiritual freedom is also found in the mind—a mind programmed with an accurate understanding of who we are based on facts and scriptural truth.

Think the Truth—About Others

"Of course I know what Janet's thinking," said Linda irritably. "I just have to look at her and I can tell." Ever found yourself saying the same thing? In our saner moments, all of us who've ever claimed we could mind-read have had to acknowledge it just isn't true. But, nevertheless, we make judgments about others based on flimsy logic.

Is what we think about others really important? Does it matter if we draw quick conclusions about someone's character or motives based on a few comments they have made? Or, even worse, based on our "intuition" about them? If we want to grow more like Jesus, what we think about others certainly is important.

Sowing seeds of suspicion and strife between people is the mark of the Enemy. He began with Eve, causing her to question God's love and good purposes for her, and he's continued his work ever since.

In talking about the devil, Bible commentators describe him as "the chief opposer of God, the archenemy who leads all the spiritual hosts of darkness. In a day of rising occultism and open Satanism, it is easier to believe the Bible's plain witness to him than twenty years ago."[3] We are naïve to think he is no longer active.

How can we spot Satan's activity? Just look for rifts in relationships and you'll see evidence of his presence. If you're married, have you ever felt your husband doesn't show enough appreciation? After all, you chase the kids all day, pick up constantly, cook, feed hungry little mouths (or big ravenous ones), race here and there to make sure everyone is happy; then your hubby comes home and says, "What did you do all day?" Brood on this or other potential flash points day after day, and Satan has fertile ground for sowing seeds of strife and discord.

Satan's activity isn't limited to the domestic front. How about conflict between family members, within your local church fellowship, in your workplace, or between friends? Using people to carry out his agenda of sowing disunity and discouragement, Satan likes nothing better than to find someone who will cooperate with him. Tempting us to comment negatively, repeating tales we've heard but not verified, or making unfair comparisons are all ways the Enemy employs us in his schemes.

Once again, our minds form the battlefield. Will we let them be Satan's "gotcha" place or guard them so they become God's growing place? Despite the Enemy's power, never forget—we're not helpless in this battle! We don't have to let Satan lodge his thoughts of suspicion and judgment in our minds. Even if you've thought things about others you'd never admit, you don't have to continue that kind of mental pattern.

Growth is God's idea—transformation is His goal. And He's provided the weapons we need for success. What are they? Once again: Examine what you tell yourself, learn to reject untrue and destructive thoughts about others, and renew your mind with truth from the Word.

1. *Examine what you tell yourself about others.* Do you find yourself ticked off at other people, chewing them out, and accusing them of various kinds of malicious motives—in your mind? Do you filter certain people's words or actions through a preconceived grid—that they are unreliable, not to be trusted, out for themselves, uncaring... ?

What kinds of things do you tell yourself about a particular person or group of people you don't get along with?

Too often our assumptions color what we see and hear. Instead of accepting actions or words at face value, we look for hidden agendas.

Whatever the provocation we face, we're called to think well of others. But let's be honest. Most of us find it tough not to think negatively about a few nameless dragons in our lives. So does that mean it's okay—we don't have to change our thinking about them? Sorry.

Remember that God's in the process of making us what we're not at this time. Therefore, change is essential if we want to progress spiritually. His Word tells us what He expects and will enable us to do: Think the truth about others, put off falsehood, speak truthfully (Ephesians 4:25). Doing this is for our own good *and* the greater good of God's kingdom. Not only will we find ourselves freed from bitterness, but God's love and concern for that nameless dragon in our life can then flow through us. No wonder Satan presses us to stubbornly hold on to our negative opinions and grudges.

To progress spiritually, we have to make a determined decision to erase, not embrace, negative thinking about others. We can't afford to make excuses and ignore the damage this causes. But how can we fight this very human tendency to mentally criticize, judge, and condemn? Some first steps in this direction involve cultivating new habits. Train yourself to ask the following questions:

Could I be wrong about the person? Do I have all of the facts? Am I biased in some way?

Am I labeling the other person, not believing they can grow and change?

Am I mind-reading, assuming I know why someone spoke or acted a certain way?

Am I magnifying the issue because of my own unacknowledged attitudes?

Do any of these questions apply to your situation? Jot down your response.

2. *Probe your emotions.* Our feelings toward other people can come from our thoughts and assumptions about them, the situation we're in, or something connected to our past that they unwittingly triggered. Have you ever instinctively felt cool toward a person because he or she reminded you of someone you disliked years before? Have you felt irritated by some innocent action, recognizing later it was linked to a long-forgotten event?

Lying in bed one morning, I grew irritated at the sound of Jim's coughing. "Why are you coughing like that?" I called through the closed bathroom door.

"I'm just clearing my lungs," Jim responded in an injured voice. "Is there a problem?"

Yes, there was a problem! In a flash I recognized my mother's tone of voice and even her very words. She hated my father's smoking habit and regularly complained about his constant cough. Decades later this totally unconnected, very distant memory had subconsciously triggered my irritation with Jim. Recognizing this spurred a quick apology, beginning the day on a happier note.

Our emotions give us messages—and we grow in maturity if we stop to probe them. Like peeling an onion, examining the outer layer won't reveal what's hidden inside. Layer after layer of assumptions, preconceived ideas, and prejudices often need to be peeled away before the core of our problem surfaces.

In our search for truth about our thoughts and feelings toward others, we need to keep probing like David: "Why are you downcast [angry, embarrassed, hurt, bitter], O my soul? Why so disturbed within me?" (Psalm 42:5). Here are some helpful questions to ask yourself as you begin this process:

What am I feeling? Anger, hurt, rejection, insecurity, insignificance?

Anger often covers other emotions, so keep probing:

Where is my anger coming from—frustration, fear, blocked goals, an inability to control a person or situation, embarrassment, guilt, or something else?

Why do I feel this way? What am I telling myself that is producing these feelings?

Are my feelings based on facts or assumptions?

Pray for insight and a willingness to be honest with yourself. Then write down what the Holy Spirit brings to your mind.

3. *Decide what action to take.* Much as we wish that difficult relationships would take care of themselves, they rarely do. God calls us, as part of His plan for our growth, to look at our thinking and the part it plays in fractured relationships and then to do something about it. Mature and effective living means learning to solve problems. When we harbor resentful thoughts, we have a spiritual and emotional problem. To stamp out these ungodly thoughts and replace them with ones that please the Lord, practice the following:

Identify and name the problem and its causes—including your own behavior. Be as specific as possible.

Determine your attitude and action. Assume the best (not the worst) about the person. Be open to the fact that you might have misunderstood their motives. Accept the truth that people have genuinely different ways of seeing things.

Consider realistic options. Ask yourself, "Is this a real problem or just a passing incident?" Is the issue worth investing the effort to resolve, or can you accept it and let it go? If, after prayer and examination of your own part in the problem, you can't let it go, do what Jesus taught. Go to the person and resolve it (Matthew 5:23-24; 18:15-17). Try to influence and change the situation for the better by problem solving, negotiating, or speaking the truth in love.

When you recognize that what you're telling yourself about someone else is negative and based on hurt or biased feelings, silently shout, "Stop!" (You could say this out loud if no one is around.) Then challenge yourself by asking, *Am I thinking what is true, noble, right, pure, lovely, and admirable?* If the answer is "No, it's not even close," go back to God and tell Him, "Lord, I want to do what pleases You but I can't do this on my own. Help!" And He will.

Learning to bring all our thoughts into captivity to Christ is part of our growth process—and can only happen with the help of the Holy Spirit. But, if we choose to cooperate with Him, we'll see some exciting changes in how we think about people and relate to them.

Think the Truth—About God

How would you complete the sentence: God is _____? If someone asked you, "What do you really think about God?" what would you say? See if you recognize your thoughts in the following true-life examples:

"God must be punishing me for something," exclaimed

John as a flashing red light and ear-piercing siren signaled him to pull over.

"Why would God let someone come to my house on the one day it was a mess and the dishes were stacked in the sink?" complained Katherine.

"I had a rotten attitude about a situation I was in," said Linda, "so I waited for God to make me feel horribly guilty because I deserved it."

How would you react in these situations? Do you see God as a killjoy, out to spoil your fun? Do you think He's like Pharaoh, demanding more than you're capable of and punishing you if you don't measure up? Is He secretly a "Top Cop," ready to zap you? Or maybe you inwardly think of Him as a celestial Santa Claus, obliged to hand out goodies because, after all, you've done all you possibly could to be perfect?

Sometimes our ideas about God bear little resemblance to the person revealed through Scripture. When this is the case, we're the losers. Distorted and inaccurate thinking about God takes away our joy, peace, sense of security, and intimacy—all qualities that cause us to spiritually flourish. After all, how can we feel joyful while waiting for God to read us the riot act? How can we delight in His acceptance when condemnation is our constant companion?

In contrast, feast your mind on one of the many descriptions of God. "Let him who boasts boast about this: that he understands and knows me, that I am the Lord, who exercises kindness, justice and righteousness on earth, for in these I delight" (Jeremiah 9:24). Keep mulling over more truths about God found in every part of Scripture. He is "the God who gives endurance and encouragement ... the God of hope ... the Father of compassion and the God of all comfort ... the God of peace" (Romans 15:5, 13; 2 Corinthians 1:3; Hebrews 13:20). What difference does an accurate view of God make in our daily lives? It opens the door to purposeful, joyful, and meaningful living.

God's true identity is revealed in careful study of the Bible and in embracing what it says. After all, without the Bible, what do we have to guide us? Yet, even among Christians, distorted ideas about God abound.

Thinking the truth about God's nature and attitude toward us is vital for our spiritual and emotional well-being. He wants us to know Him and enjoy His presence. To help us do that, let's examine the four erroneous ideas about God already mentioned— ideas any of us can trip over.

Common Distortions

The Killjoy God. Do you imagine God leaning down from heaven and shouting, "Cut out that fun. Stop laughing. Don't you know life is serious?" When life's going well, do you begin to dread that something's going to go wrong because God's going to spoil it? If you do, then you're actually believing a lie— but you're not alone in thinking this.

Not only do some Christians think that following God means being deadly serious about everything, they also give this impression to others. Even more damaging is the belief we can pass on to our children: to be a Christian is to live a dour, sour, and fun-less life.

How do you convey the joy of your relationship with Jesus to those around you? To your children? And, if you're married to a nonbeliever, what ideas about God does he absorb from living with you? People sometimes look at Christianity and think, "What a drab way to live." Why? Could it be we're giving that impression? Do they see God as a killjoy—someone who grimly condemns us to a stale, sterile life void of any sizzle and snap?

Using human terms, the Bible reveals God as a person with emotions ranging all the way from love to wrath to deep yearning. We're also told we are made in His image. So, wouldn't this God also laugh and rejoice as we do? James writes the truth: "Don't be deceived.... Every good and perfect gift is from above" (James 1:17). Laughter, enjoyment, and creativity are all good gifts from God.

I can imagine God chuckling as He observed one little boy that I heard about. Squirming on the front row of a small southern church, the child refused to sit quietly and pay attention. His frustrated father finally decided he'd had enough. Tucking his small son under his arm, he marched down the aisle while trying to ignore the understanding looks of all the other parents. Suddenly everyone's attention was riveted on them as the little boy cried out in a charming southern accent, "Y'all pray for me now."

God is not a sourpuss. He's given us laughter, which is medicine to our bones (Proverbs 17:22). Get rid of the damaging idea that Christians follow a killjoy God. He's a God who calls us to celebrate, sing, rejoice, or simply make cheerful noises if that's the extent of our musical ability. Laugh, dance, delight yourself in Him—our God of joy.

The Pharaoh God. Speaking at a counseling conference several years ago, pastor and author David Seamans discussed the distorted ways in which we view God. He described the Pharaoh God as one who lashes out at us in our minds, demanding more and more, just as the Egyptian Pharaoh made cruel demands of the Israelite slaves. Do you live under this misconception? Do you feel you never measure up, you can never do enough to please God or to keep in His good favor?

Years after I had become a Christian, these thoughts came into my mind. I was busy teaching the Word, yet my mind was filled with the idea that I could never be or do enough to please God. The accusations came: *You don't pray enough; you don't give enough; you don't witness enough. You're just not who you should be.* "God," I cried out, "I can never be enough."

Ever felt that way? That you just can't make it? You just can't measure up to God's impossible standards and therefore can never please Him? What a distortion this is of our relationship with God! Paul writes, "It is by grace you have been saved, through faith—

117

and this not from yourselves, it is the gift of God—not by works, so that no one can boast" (Ephesians 2:8-9).

If you know you're driven or depressed by your relationship with God, ask yourself if you see Him as a Pharaoh—unfair, overly demanding, never satisfied. If you do, you've been following a distortion.

God didn't reach out to you with a long list of what you must do to be accepted, but with grace—unearned, undeserved mercy and love. And that's how we still find favor and acceptance in His sight. We can't earn it, and we don't have to try. We don't have to live under any harrowing inner command to do more and more. He has accepted us completely—so relax and rejoice in this truth.

The Policeman God. This is the God who is waiting to pounce on you. He's watching your every move and when He sees you doing something wrong He's going to yell, "I saw you speeding." "I saw you grinding your teeth in frustration at your child." "I saw your attitude toward your husband." "I saw your behavior at work." "You're going to pay for this." What is our reaction to this distorted view of God's character? Instead of being glad that God sees all we face in life, we shrink back in fear, waiting for some divine punishment to make us miserable.

The truth is, God does see us. He sees everything. But why does He observe all our ways? And what is His attitude as He sees us going through our daily lives? Is it to punish us, to "zap" us, to give us a good whack when we step out of line? Or is He looking at us with the delighted, loving, concerned eyes of a perfect parent?

I'm far from being a perfect parent, but when my son or daughter comes home to visit, I watch them with delight and joy. In fact, I feast my eyes on them because I miss them so much. I'm not looking to see what they're doing wrong. Likewise, God doesn't look at us to spot our flaws or remind us of our failings.

We find a beautiful picture of how God observes us in Psalm 139. David cries out with joyful assurance, "Where can I go from your Spirit? Where can I flee from your presence? If I go up to the heavens, you are there; if I make my bed in the depths, you are there. If I rise on the wings of the dawn, if I settle on the far side of the sea, even there your hand will guide me, your right hand will hold me fast" (vv. 7-10).

There's no hiding from God. He sees both our failings and our good points. But He doesn't watch with the intention of punishing us. Instead, as David declares, God is there to guide and hold us with His hand of power—not to get us, or to stomp on us. Do you believe this?

The Santa Claus God. This is the belief that God sees whether we've been naughty or nice and pours out life's goodies in proportion to how good we've been. After all, if we've done the right things, had our devotions most days, given to the Salvation Army, or helped lick envelopes in the church office once in a while, surely God should make our lives go smoothly. Nothing awful should ever happen to us because we've been so good.

If we subscribe to this distortion, however, when God does allow testings and trials, it's easy to get really mad at Him. Have you ever thought, *God, this isn't fair. I've served You so well all these years, yet You've allowed _____ (fill in the blank) to happen.* Or, *How could You do this to me when I've done so much for You?* If you have these thoughts, you've bought into the Santa Claus image of God.

Striking bargains with us isn't God's way. We're called to live for Him out of gratitude and love for all He's done, but that doesn't guarantee our lives will always be smooth and easy. There is no Santa Claus God. But Scripture tells us of someone far greater— the Almighty, All-Sufficient, and All-Loving God, who lavishly pours out abundant spiritual blessings, sufficient for every situation we face.

Does it matter what we think? Without a doubt. Turn the spotlight on your thought life. It holds the key to finding freedom from negative self-talk, fractured relationships, and fears about how God views us. Guard what goes into your gray cells—make sure that it's the truth about yourself, other people, and God. If it isn't—toss it out!

Remember, what you think about *does* matter. Not only do our thoughts hinder or help us to become what we're not, they determine our attitudes. And wouldn't you rather go through life with positive, life-changing attitudes than petty, life-spoiling ones? I know I would.

Reflections—for Thought and Discussion

1. How would you answer the question *Does it matter what I think?* What important principles do you find in the following verses about the use of our minds: Ephesians 4:22-24; Colossians 3:2; 2 Peter 3:1; James 4:1?

2. Do you ever give yourself an inner tongue-lashing? What do you tell yourself at these times? How does your self-labeling measure up against God's statements about you?

3. Where do you think your negative messages come from? What's your response mentally and emotionally when they come into your mind?

4. What practical lessons did you gain from the section *Think the Truth About Yourself?* Did one stand out in particular? Why do you think this is so?

5. What do you sometimes find yourself thinking about other people? How does the section *Think the Truth About Others* help or challenge you in this area?

6. Did you identify with any of the distortions mentioned in *Think the Truth About God?* What steps could you begin to take now to replace them with a biblical view of God?

Memory Verse

"May the words of my mouth and the meditation of my heart be pleasing in your sight, O Lord, my Rock and my Redeemer" (Psalm 19:14).

Notes:

1 Elizabeth George, *Loving God With All Your Mind* (Eugene, Ore.: Harvest House Publishers, 1994), 14.

2 Neil Anderson, *The Bondage Breaker* (Eugene, Ore.: Harvest House Publishers, 1990), 52.

3 Kenneth L. Barker and John R. Kohlenberger III, *NIV Bible Commentary, Volume 2: New Testament* (Grand Rapids, Mich.: Zondervan Publishing House, 1994), 19.

SEVEN

You Mean, I Have to Change My Attitude?

"I'M HAVING A VERY DIFFICULT TIME GETTING MY LESSON DONE each week," I moaned to the other women in my small group Bible study. "My children are up and running as soon as I am. There's no way I can have a quiet time."

Several other young mothers nodded their heads in empathy. "We know what you mean," they chorused.

"Well, I don't think you should have a problem," said Denise. "I was raised with the saying 'No Bible, no breakfast.' If you disciplined yourself not to read the newspaper or eat breakfast before doing your Bible study, you wouldn't have a problem."

Needless to say, I didn't smile warmly and thank her for such insightful advice.

What does she know? I fumed to myself later. *She doesn't even have any children. Who does she think she is—trying to tell me how to juggle kids and do my Bible study first thing in the morning?*

Sitting in class the next week, I noticed Denise was absent. Still rankled by her comments, I was glad she hadn't come—until I found out why. Denise had been asked into the leadership group and would be a new discussion leader. I was even more irritated.

Why would they choose her? I asked myself. *After all, she has no empathy with anyone. Look how she spoke to me. I certainly wouldn't want to be in her class.*

Hours later, my insides still churned with irritation at the news of Denise's new opportunity. But the next day during my prayer time,

God had something to say to me. "Poppy," came the loud yet loving voice of the Holy Spirit, "you're jealous. That's what is really eating at you. You want to be invited into leadership also." Ouch.

Long ago God caused another woman to say more than "ouch" when her jealousy led to criticism of God's chosen leader. Miriam, Moses' older sister, felt he was getting an unfair share of glory. After inwardly stewing, she sniped to Aaron, and both went public with their sour feelings.

"'Has the Lord spoken only through Moses?' they asked. 'Hasn't he also spoken through us?'" (Numbers 12:2).

God's anger burned against Miriam for her jealous criticism—she would not go unpunished. White with leprosy, Miriam humbly observed the true greatness of Moses as he pleaded with God to heal her. Who could blame Moses if he'd secretly thought, "Thank You, God, for putting her in her place." But clearly he didn't. Seven days of public humiliation taught Miriam a mighty lesson. Jealousy is an ugly offense in God's eyes. When allowed to take root and spread, it divides and destroys marriages, friendships, and the family of God. "But," we squirm, "isn't it just part of being human?"

I'm Only Human

Admitting we aren't perfect isn't all that hard for most of us. Usually, however, we're careful not to let others know the details of what's eating us. "I'm feeling down," we say. Or "I got up on the wrong side of the bed." Or "I'm a bit grouchy but I'll get over it." Often we don't want to admit even to ourselves what's really deep down inside. When we do, it's cushioned by the consoling thought *I'm only human.*

Like it or not, we *are* human—and because of this, at one time or another we do find ourselves nursing attitudes we'd rather no one knew about. Once we realize what's going on inside us, our human instinct is to hide, just as Adam and Eve hid from God in the Garden. Like them, we grab for any excuse—and usually find many.

1. "I'm only human." Translation: *It's human nature to feel like this.*

2. "I'm no different." Translation: *Everyone has negative attitudes toward people, so why shouldn't I?*

3. "It doesn't matter." Translation: *What's the harm?*

4. "I'll deal with it later." Translation: *It isn't important enough to deal with now.*

5. "They made me feel/act this way." Translation: *If they hadn't, I wouldn't have. They are to blame for my attitude, not me.*

Do you recognize these? Are there others you're familiar with? Write them down.

Making excuses for attitudes that come from our old nature feels good. That's why we cling to them. But the truth is, when jealousy, pushiness, and a pouty or petty spirit are allowed to take root, we become spiritually infected. Instead of being spiritually healthy, our vitality and joy in the Lord slowly ebbs away. And, not only are we affected by these fleshly attitudes, our infection can spread to others as well.

Candid Camera—Bible Style

Have you ever wondered why the Bible is crammed with hundreds of stories about people just like us? After all, God could have filled Scripture with pure doctrine. Or perfect people. As our Creator, however, He knows we learn best from real-life stories of people's mistakes and successes rather than dry theory.

Considering the biblical truth that we are all born with a sin nature, it's not surprising to see how many people mentioned in Scripture had attitude problems like ours. Some, however, inspire and teach us through their mature handling of their human disposition toward sin.

The Bible doesn't whitewash people's attitudes or actions. Instead, the writers paint them in bold, broad strokes so we won't miss either the warnings or the examples God intends. In our journey toward becoming more like the Lord, we can profit from both. Out of the many people whose lives could teach us powerful lessons, we'll look at six. Three messed up. Three showed mature attitudes that reflect their convictions about God. We'll begin with Pushy Sarai, Pouty Ahab, and Petty Haman.

Pushy Sarai. Attitude: "I'll Do It My Way."

Can't you imagine Sarai stomping her foot and telling Abram, "I've waited long enough. I've had as much as I can take. Obviously God has kept me from bearing you a child, so let's just sort the problem out by ourselves"? Being a loving, long-term husband, Abram knew better than to ignore his wife.

Although we can't tell for sure from her words, Sarai's attitude seems tinged with resentment and desperation. Waiting year after year, her patience and faith that God would give them a child had slowly evaporated. When God doesn't act on our timetable, what can we do but come up with our own plan?

Knowing that the customs of her day permitted a female servant to act as a surrogate mother, Sarai made a proposition to Abram. Perhaps the conversation went something like this:

"Look, Abram, Mrs. Jones who lives in the camp down the road couldn't have any children, either. She suggested to Mr. Jones that he have a child through her maid, and now she's the mother of a bouncing baby boy. Abram, couldn't we do this? Please, please?"

For some strange reason we don't hear Abram protesting. He did as Sarai suggested and, indeed, in due time they did have a bouncing baby boy through Hagar. But they also reaped consequences that affect the world to this day (Genesis 16:1-6).

Faithless Attitudes

When what we want doesn't happen, it's easy to step in and take control. Who of us isn't familiar with pushing, nagging, whining, or even withholding affection if that's what it takes to get our way? But pushy and impatient attitudes don't rise out of thin air. They come from our thoughts and beliefs—from what we tell ourselves about our circumstances and from our view of God.

Sarai believed, accurately, that God had prevented her from getting pregnant. But she then leapt to the conclusion that she would never have a child. The truth was, of course, that God had a different timing in mind to fit His greater purpose. When we're in God's waiting room—whether it's for a new job, a life partner, a happier relationship with the partner we have, or a prodigal child's turnaround—our thinking and attitudes can get as messed up as Sarai's.

"Why doesn't God do something?" we fuss and fume. "Obviously He doesn't care. Maybe this isn't a big enough problem for His attention. Or perhaps it's true that 'God helps those who help themselves.' I guess I'll just have to take charge and make things happen my way." And away we go, hacking at people's feelings, backing them into a corner till they agree to what we want, manipulating circumstances, and causing our victims to run when they spy us steaming toward them.

What do we reveal with this behavior? Underneath a pushy, impatient attitude and the need to control people and events there lies something deeper. Pushiness means fear and worry have us by the throat. It reveals that we have temporarily lost our trust and confidence in God.

Take a few moments to reflect on areas of frustration in your life—places where you find yourself impatiently pushing people or manipulating circumstances to get what you want. To help you face and fight this fleshly infection, record any situation(s) where you find yourself tempted to think, "God doesn't seem to be in control, so I'd better make sure everything goes as it should."

In contrast to our faithless attitudes, let's see how we can respond in a more positive and life-changing way.

Mature Responses

A motto hanging on the office wall of a famous missionary startled many of his visitors. It said, "Why pray when you can worry?"[1] Isn't that too often our reaction to frustrations and fears? But what does God urge us to do instead? Over and over we're told to trust Him.

"Trust in the Lord with all your heart and lean not on your own understanding; in all your ways acknowledge him, and he will make your paths straight" (Proverbs 3:5-6).

Trusting God is like relying on the chair you're sitting in. You have *confidence* your chair will hold you up, not dump you unceremoniously on the floor. Your confidence then allows you to *depend* on the chair, to lean your whole weight on it. By sitting in the chair, you're exercising your *faith* that the chair that sustained you yesterday will hold you up today and tomorrow.

Trusting God involves these same attitudes: *confidence* that He will hold you up spiritually and emotionally through the waiting time; *dependence* on His wisdom and timing; and *faith* that He is an unchanging God who keeps His promises. Breaking the pattern of pushing for our way and our timing is possible when we learn to trust God. Another help in our struggle to trust and wait is realizing that even though we can't see what He's doing, God has His reasons for making us wait. Here are some to think about:

• Sometimes circumstances aren't yet in place for what God intends to do.

• God is working in another person, and we need to wait for that work to be accomplished.

• God has a greater purpose than what we're praying for. He's going to surprise us!

• God wants to develop some quality(s) in us first. *We* are not ready yet for *His* plans.

Sarai pushed ahead of God's timing *and* God's way of answering her heart's desire. Most of us have probably done the same thing and have our share of regrets. Whatever mistakes we've made as a result of a pushy and impatient spirit, let's rejoice in the fact that we can grow and learn from past failings. When our fleshly nature rises up and says, "I've got to take control because God isn't acting fast enough," let's remind ourselves to do three things:

• Calm down.

• Focus on God's character and promises.

• Consciously choose to trust His goodness and wisdom.

Pouty Ahab. Attitude: "Life's Not Fair."

"What on earth is the matter?" demanded Jezebel, wife of King Ahab. Lying on his bed sulking, Ahab moaned, "I asked Naboth to sell me his vineyard, or to trade it, and he refused."

Like a little boy who couldn't have dessert until he'd finished his vegetables, Ahab no doubt thought, *Life's not fair. Why can't I have my own way?* By passing on his self-pitying attitude to his nothing-can-stand-in-my-way wife, Ahab eventually got what he wanted. After arranging for Naboth's death, Jezebel wasted no time dragging Ahab from his bed and hustling him down to claim the coveted vineyard. But his pleasure was short-lived. Elijah, God's spokesman, soon confronted him: "The Lord is going to bring great harm to you and sweep you away...." (1 Kings 21:1-24 TLB).

Faithless Attitudes

Did anyone promise us life would be fair? That we'd always be treated the way we want to be treated? Or that we'd be able to get whatever would make us happy? The temptation to pout, stomp our feet, and mutter, "Life isn't fair," springs from many sources.

When I visited a new doctor recently, I had to fill out a routine but thorough health questionnaire. "Put a check beside any health problem you have had or are currently being treated for," the office assistant instructed. The questionnaire covered everything from problems with your heart, kidneys, and lungs to diseases I'd never heard of. In spite of my best efforts over the years to exercise, munch apples, eat broccoli, and even chew on Styrofoam disks masquerading as rice cakes, I still had a depressing number of check marks on my paper.

Is life fair? No. Would lying on my bed sulking and complaining to God improve the situation? Nope. Will it improve your situation? Not at all likely. There is something, however, that does cure those "poor me" feelings we all wrestle with— resting in the truth that nothing happens to us without divine permission, and that "God works for the good of those who love him" (Romans 8:28).

Sometimes we aim our ugly mood at God, but much of the time we direct it at people around us. We want our way even in minor issues such as eating at the restaurant *we* prefer, catching a particular movie on the night *we* want to go, or getting control of the remote so *we* decide what program to watch. What's our response when this doesn't happen? Does it bear a sneaking resemblance to Ahab's? How about on bigger issues?

Think about the last time you had a good pout or felt life wasn't fair. What was the issue? Is it a habitual response? Write down what comes to mind.

Even though we don't like to admit it, when we pout because our wants aren't put first, we're being self-centered. Most of us are highly alert to our own needs and desires, but it's easy to either ignore the preferences of others or not care whether their needs are met. Ugh! The truth isn't pleasant, is it?

What can we do? A first step is to take seriously the words found in Hebrews, "Let us throw off *everything* that hinders and the sin that so easily entangles" (12:1, emphasis added). With the Holy Spirit's help, we can keep from hugging habit patterns that belong to our old nature.

Mature Responses

What's the opposite of self-centeredness? A sensitivity to others. But snapping the chains of self-centeredness that lie at the root of pouty attitudes is something only God can do— although we do have a part to play.

When my daughter, Malaika, was in kindergarten, I felt convicted about my attitude toward her. She was a sweet child, but because of my own struggles at that season of life, frustration and anger sometimes spilled over into our relationship. As I prayed about this one morning, God impressed on me the dangers that might lie ahead for her if she didn't feel secure in my love. Weeping before the Lord in repentance, I pleaded with Him to change my heart and actions.

The next day, while reading a book in the family room, Malaika called from the bathroom, "Mommy, come and soap me." Instantly, irritation at having to stop doing what I enjoyed flared up. But just as fast, I sensed the Holy Spirit saying, "Poppy, yesterday you pleaded for a changed heart. Here's your opportunity to prove you meant it. Put your book down, get up, and go help her. She doesn't want to be soaped, she wants to be loved." I could have pouted and procrastinated but I'm so glad I didn't. In God's lovingkindness, that moment became a new beginning.

Honesty with ourselves and God propels us to earnest prayer for a changed heart. But more than this is required. When the Spirit opens up opportunities to act in new ways, we must say yes. Otherwise our tearful pleadings are empty words, not sincere longings. As we walk step by step with the Lord in this way, growth into the likeness of Christ happens.

How might opportunities to act in new ways come in your life? It might mean accepting your husband's need to rest when you're ready to paint the town—or at least head to the paint store. It could mean giving more time to your child when you'd rather do something else. It might require sacrificing your lunch hour to help a new colleague feel at home.

My close friend Carol demonstrates sensitivity to others at her church most Sundays. "Sure, I'd love to spend the coffee break between services chatting with my friends," she comments. "But I find it hard to ignore people standing around by themselves looking lost. I reach out to them because I know church can be a lonely place until you get hooked up with others."

Our supreme model of sensitivity to the needs of others is, of course, the Lord himself. Can you imagine Him pouting when the disciples made no move to wash His feet? Taking a towel, He humbled himself, sensitively meeting their needs (and teaching them a major lesson at the same time). Pointing to Christ as our example, Paul writes, "Look not only to your own interests, but also to the interests of others" (Philippians 2:4).

Whose interests do we seek? When we pout to get our way or to punish others, aren't we seeking our own—just like Ahab? Let's make it our goal, instead, to cultivate sensitivity to the needs of others, starting with our families. How about looking for ways to do this at work, too, and in our church fellowships?

Instead of slamming doors, sticking out our lip, or sliding into icy silence, let's ditch the pouty, self-centered attitude that whimpers, "*Life's* not fair. *He's* not fair. *She's* not fair. *They* aren't fair. *Why can't I have my way?*" Our goal is to grow in maturity, which we can embrace as a lifelong process. We'll be taking one giant step toward this goal when we start praying, "Dear Lord, please help me to not sulk when I can't get my way. Help me, instead, to focus on understanding and meeting the needs of _____."

Petty Haman. Attitude: "You're Making Me Unhappy."

"Can you believe all the great things happening to me?" asked Haman excitedly. Crowded around him, his wife and friends listened eagerly. "I have piles of money, many sons, and the king has elevated me above everyone else. But even more than that, I was the only person Queen Esther invited to accompany the king to the banquet she gave. And she invited me to come back tomorrow as well."

Even as he enjoyed the admiring comments and envious looks of those in the room, Haman's face darkened. Glowering, he continued, "But all this gives me no satisfaction as long as I see that Jew Mordecai sitting at the king's gate" (Esther 5:9-14, author's paraphrase).

In view of how well everything was going for him, what spoiled Haman's supreme moment of glory? Why was his joy ruined by one little man? Mordecai, a God-fearing Jew, wouldn't bow down to him—it was *his* fault Haman's happiness was ruined.

Tormented by Mordecai's refusal to acknowledge his power and position, Haman let this insignificant situation irritate him beyond endurance. His pettiness proved to be his downfall.

Faithless Attitudes

It's easy to blame others for our unhappiness. Have you ever heard yourself saying, "If *you* hadn't done that, I wouldn't have said what I did." "If *you* would keep your room picked up, I wouldn't nag like I do." "If *you* ..." In other words, life would be wonderful if only this irritant were removed.

What is pettiness? It's magnifying the minor and ignoring the major. It's focusing on the little thing that isn't quite right in my life or in someone else's personality or habits—and ignoring all that is good. It's blowing up small stuff and minimizing what's more important. When a petty attitude grips us, we build up a head of steam over issues that mean nothing in the larger scheme of life.

How can we spot this attitude in ourselves? Here are three areas to watch:

Outside the home: Think about how you interact with people where you work, serve, or attend classes. Are you quicker to notice and comment on someone's minor flaws—or their major positive qualities?

In your marriage: In a survey of male/female relationships, Shere Hite noted women complained that men interrupt, seem not to really hear or be aware of the hurts they cause, and use condescending, judgmental attitudes toward them.[2] Intimate relationships are often rocky, given the fact they are formed between two imperfect people. Do we choose, then, to focus on the flaws and failings we wish our spouse didn't have, blaming him for our unhappiness? Or will we close our eyes when we need to, pick up the socks, speak through the newspaper, and keep reminding ourselves of all the good traits he possesses?

With your children: "Sit up straight." "Hold your fork properly." "Get that room cleaned up." All these normal motherly instructions seem so reasonable to us. But do our corrections outweigh our positive comments? Could we be magnifying minor issues as a mom and, in our pettiness, be creating resentful feelings in our kids?

Haman found little comfort or joy from all the good things in his life. In the end, his obsessive need to have everything his way cost him all he had. How about us? Don't we want good working relationships with others? Enriching friendships? Happy marriages? Contented families? Could we be undermining all that we have because of our petty obsession with people's minor flaws or different habits?

Reflect on your relationships. Do you see a petty attitude creeping in?

Jot down any areas that need further thought, prayer, or action.

Mature Responses

How do we overcome a tendency to be petty and blame others for our unhappiness? The key doesn't lie in the other person changing, because we have no control over that (although we can keep sweetly plugging away with our children—and we can try some friendly negotiating with our spouses). The answer really lies in our cultivating different attitudes toward *them*.

Instead of responding like Haman and allowing a petty attitude to provoke us to anger, God wants us to develop tolerance and patience with others. Paul urges, "Clothe yourselves with ... patience. Bear with each other and forgive whatever grievances you may have against one another" (Colossians 3:12-13).

Being tolerant of someone doesn't imply agreement with their views or behavior. Nor does it mean we appreciate all their personality traits. A godly tolerance teaches us to accept their right to think or act differently from us—and to refrain from finding fault with them because of this. Tolerance is allowing another person to be who they are, enjoy what they enjoy, and take their own responsibility for how they live.

We might grow in tolerating someone whose personality or behavior irritates us, but what if they keep it up? Aren't we justified in blaming them for upsetting us, like Haman did? Growing spiritually strong demands we work on cultivating patience. Why? Because God is infinitely patient with our feelings, flaws, and failings. He is slow to anger. To be more like Him means we, too, need to develop patience and slowness to anger with others.

Jerry Bridges, author of *The Practice of Godliness* states, "The best way to develop this slowness to anger is to reflect frequently on the patience of God toward us."[3] Think about how patient God has been with you—then ask Him to help you deal with any tendency to be nitpicky, petty, and impatient. You won't be the only one who's glad to see this attitude left behind.

Now that we've had our eyes opened to faithless attitudes that might infect our lives, we'll turn our attention to three inspiring role models. None of these three had easy lives, yet their attitudes have much to teach us. Let's see what we can learn for our own spiritual growth from Positive Esther, Persevering Paul, and Praiseful Mary.

Positive Esther. Attitude: "God Is With Me."

"This girl has to come with me to the king's palace," an official no doubt barked to a heartbroken Mordecai. King Xerxes was on the hunt for a new wife, and this meant hundreds of young virgins being rounded up and herded into his harem. Esther, a beautiful young Jewish girl, could not escape. Whatever girlish dreams she'd had about the boy next door or having her own home and family were dashed in an instant.

Once in the harem, Esther had a choice. She could respond with tears, wailing, bitter words, and a hostile spirit. Or she could reject self-pity, hopelessness, a sour spirit, and a victim mentality. How did she react when she found herself in a situation she didn't want? She chose a positive attitude. Because of this, the Bible states that Esther pleased everyone she met and won the favor and approval of the king (Esther 2:1-17).

Esther faced the same kinds of choices you and I confront when we're caught in situations we don't like. We can push, pout, and be petty, or choose to be positive—feeding our faith on the promise that God is not only with us, He's also in control and has a purpose in mind. Oswald Chambers, author of *My Utmost for His Highest*, writes, "A spiritually vigorous saint never believes that his circumstances simply happen at random."[4]

Some situations in life can't be changed. But they have the power to change us—into a bitter victim or a victor over our loss and pain. Esther chose to be an "overcomer," to accept the unexpected and the unchangeable. She wouldn't let what had happened ruin the rest of her life.

How about us? How do we react to situations we can't control or change? Few people go through life without encountering some difficult or undesirable circumstance. You might have had a horrible experience as a child, been stung to the core by the rejection of someone you loved and trusted, or received a blow that has shaken your world. In many cases, we can't choose what happens to us, but we can choose how we react.

Will we let what has happened ruin the rest of our lives, robbing us of blessings God has in store? Will we waste the growth and opportunities for service He intends? Or will we respond as Esther did, with a positive attitude flowing from unshakable faith that God is with us in every situation? Take time to reflect on these important questions—then share your thoughts and feelings as a prayer to God.

Persevering Paul. Attitude: "God Is Good."

I wonder how many of us would keep serving God if we went through troubles, hardships, distresses, beatings, imprisonment, riots, hunger, poverty, false accusations, and even shipwreck—especially for being a follower of Christ. It's hard enough to get through little problems without diving into the dumps. We likely wouldn't cope well if we faced a fraction of the sufferings Paul encountered for the sake of the gospel.

What enabled Paul to continue despite all that he endured? To sing in prison after a savage beating? To witness to soldiers and write to believers while in a rough Roman cell?

His ability to keep living for Christ was clearly fueled by the Holy Spirit and his conviction that God is good. Paul was no superhuman, a different species from the rest of us. He, too, experienced distress, pressure, and despair (2 Corinthians 1:3-10). And in the midst of the endless difficulties he faced, he, too, had to choose his attitude.

As a spiritual role model, Paul has much to teach us about the mature Christian life. He was a man of confidence, thankfulness, and contentment—attitudes that can not only mark our lives but change them. Let's see how.

Confidence: In spite of the hardships he suffered, Paul boldly affirmed his confidence in God: "I know whom I have believed.... For to me, to live is Christ.... Now it is God who makes both us and you stand firm in Christ" (2 Timothy 1:12; Philippians 1:21; 2 Corinthians 1:21). Following his dramatic initial encounter with the Lord on the road to Damascus, Paul grew in his knowledge and experience of the living Christ. And the more he walked with Him the greater his confidence.

If you're not confident about what you believe, take action. Ask your pastor or a Christian friend where you can find the facts you need. Facing life uncertain of the God you serve will sap your confidence and hinder you from helping those who look to you for answers. But, most importantly, in addition to making time to grow in knowledge, pray for a growing intimacy with Jesus himself. Both are vital for a radiant, confident attitude.

Thankfulness: The psalmist writes, "Give thanks to the Lord, for he is good; his love endures forever (106:1). Understanding God's love as revealed in Jesus Christ caused Paul's heart to overflow with thankfulness. He thanked God constantly for the privilege of knowing and serving Him, and for those who put their faith in Christ. In turn, he admonished them—and us—to be filled with a thankful spirit.

An attitude of gratitude feeds our faith. It also honors God. He deserves our constant thanks, not only for all our external blessings but also for His personal, sustaining care each day. Paul's constant thankfulness fed his faith, making it vibrant and living, able to overcome whatever difficulty came his way.

Let's shun a grumbling, complaining spirit that flounces, "Well, I can't see anything to be thankful about." Ask God to open your eyes and soften your heart.

When this spiritual infection has been dealt with, cultivate the habit of spontaneously thanking Him. Begin in the morning as you get up, appreciating all you have. Keep on being thankful as you move through your day. Close the day by expressing gratitude to God for all the ways He has proved himself faithful. Make a conscious effort to notice things to be thankful for until thankfulness becomes a habit. Your attitude will not only strengthen your own faith, but others will be motivated by your example.

Contentment: It's tempting to believe that Paul was always a "super-saint." Could he really have struggled, as we do, to develop a mature faith? Paul never claimed to have an automatically contented heart. He confessed, in fact, that this was a growth area in his life. "I have learned the secret of being content in any and every situation," he says (Philippians 4:12). Being content with our possessions, position, or prospects in life is not a human trait—but one we need to cultivate as we grow in Christ.

Thankfulness and contentment are twin peas in a pod. When we're content, we're thankful for all God has provided. When we verbalize thankfulness, our hearts often settle into contentment. There's no place for a griping, grumbling attitude. The contented person "believes God will indeed meet all his material needs and that he will work in all his circumstances for his good."[5] But even Paul had to develop this attitude. It wasn't automatic.

Where does the power to be content come from? It grows out of the conviction that God is good and will provide what we need—not necessarily what we want or what other people have. Even though Paul went through much physical deprivation, he accepted the fact that God gives people different degrees of wealth, power, and position.

This is a challenge for each of us in our journey toward maturity. Can we graciously live with the fact that someone else's talents outshine our own? Can we be content with fewer material possessions than a friend or neighbor? Can we be content with our job/career/employment situation? Can we accept that others have more opportunities in life than we have because God has allowed it to be this way?

A lack of contentment can gnaw away at our hearts, leaving us resentful and infected spiritually. Cultivating the attitude that God is good and loves us deeply enables us to fight against the desires of our flesh. As we continue to trust God's ways in our life, we'll be able to say, like Paul, "I have learned to be content." This is a true mark of spiritual maturity.

Do you struggle with having confidence in what you believe, being thankful, or feeling content? Write down the areas where you need to grow. Pray about them and ask God to help you develop your walk with Him in these areas.

Praiseful Mary. Attitude: "God Is Worthy."

The news stunned Mary. She had been chosen to bear the Son of the Most High, and she wasn't even married. "How will this be?" she asked. After hearing the angel Gabriel's answer, Mary responded, "I am the Lord's servant, may it be to me as you have said" (Luke 1:26-38).

How easy it would have been for Mary to question, argue, focus on the obstacles, even resist what God wanted to do in her life. Instead, she willingly cooperated with the divine plan to bless the world through the birth of Jesus. While visiting her cousin Elizabeth, the soon-to-be mother of John the Baptist, Mary's joy knew no bounds. Bursting into song, she praised God for all His blessings.

"My soul glorifies the Lord and my spirit rejoices in God my Savior, for he has been mindful of the humble state of his servant. From now on all generations will call me blessed, for the Mighty One has done great things for me—holy is his name" (Luke 1:46-49). Filled with the Holy Spirit, Mary expressed her delight in God and acknowledged His great blessing in choosing her to be the mother of our Lord.

Praise is exalting God by recounting who He is and what He has done. Filling our lips with words of adoration and worship, we elevate Him to His rightful place in our hearts. A standard teaching of the church says, "The chief end of man is to glorify God and

141

enjoy Him forever."[6] When we cultivate a praiseful attitude, we *are* glorifying God and *will* enjoy Him forever.

The natural outcome of a heart that genuinely praises God, seeing Him as holy and sovereign over all, is a profound awareness that He alone is worthy of our devotion. Who else, or what other earthly objective, is worth giving our lives to? Mary grasped this and counted nothing in her life as more important than saying yes to God. No matter what the cost, she would be His servant, confident that His plans for her were shaped by divine wisdom and unconditional love.

Like Mary, our lives can sparkle with praise and adoration to God. And, by God's design, a praiseful attitude becomes a conduit of blessing, providing strength in sorrow, perspective in confusion, and encouragement in trials. Praise also lifts our eyes above our earthbound horizons and onto God's mighty purposes.

Finding ourselves more interested in serving God than ourselves is clear evidence of the Spirit's work in our attitudes. Mary's response to Gabriel's message is a powerful illustration of this. What can we learn from this as we seek to grow spiritually? The same Holy Spirit who filled Mary's heart with total devotion to God longs to do the same in us. We face the same choice she did. We can adopt an attitude that puts our plans and desires first, or we can joyfully declare, "I am the Lord's servant, may it be to me as you have said." As you consider a situation you are facing, which attitude are you choosing?

What is the key to ongoing change in our attitudes—seeing those pushy, pouty, petty responses and all their fleshly relatives swept out of our lives? There's only one answer. The Bible tells us to "be filled with the Spirit" (Ephesians 5:18). This is the only power source for changed attitudes.

You and I don't have the ability to become different people on our own. We need the Holy Spirit's help every day of our lives. And the wonderful thing is, He is available to fill us with power whatever time of day we call or wherever we are. Do we have to change our attitudes to grow more like Christ? Yes! Can we? Yes! God promises to provide all we need for life and godliness. So let's take hold of His resources and allow Him to change us.

As God transforms us into the likeness of Christ, He often uses trials and testings. What is He doing when hurts and heartaches touch our lives? Does He care? And how can we stay standing— coming through spiritually stronger than before? Let's see what we can learn to help us through this inevitable part of the journey toward maturity.

Reflections—for Thought and Discussion

1. What "less-than-perfect" attitudes have you seen in other people? (No names, please!) How about in yourself?

2. With whom do you identify the most—*Pushy Sarai, Pouty Ahab,* or *Petty Haman*? Or is there another Bible character whose reactions seem more like your own? What makes you choose this particular person?

3. Look back at the *Mature Responses* God desires that we exhibit. How are you helped or challenged by these and the Scriptures mentioned?

4. What impressed you about Esther's positive attitude in the face of difficult circumstances? How can you apply this to a situation in your life?

5. Paul suffered a great deal yet never doubted that God was good. What can you learn from his attitude?

6. What does Mary's praiseful attitude teach you about being open to God's surprises? What attitude will you choose if God surprises you this week?

Memory Verse

"He died for all, that those who live should no longer live for themselves but for him who died for them and was raised again" (2 Corinthians 5:15).

Notes:

1 J. Oswald Sanders, *In Pursuit of Maturity* (Grand Rapids, Mich.: Zondervan Publishing House, 1986), 106.

2 Shere Hite, quoted in *The Sunday Oregonian* (October 18, 1987).

3 Jerry Bridges, *The Practice of Godliness* (Colorado Springs, Colo.:NavPress, 1983), 207.

4 Oswald Chambers, *My Utmost for His Highest* (Grand Rapids, Mich.: Discovery House Publishers, RBC Ministries, 1995), July 11 entry.

5 Jerry Bridges, *The Practice of Godliness*, 106.

6 Westminster Catechism.

EIGHT

How Can I Stand in Life's Storms?

"I THINK YOU KNEW MY MOTHER," SAID JUNE, A YOUNG MISSIONARY to Europe. As we talked, I remembered her mother had been a gifted small group leader in her church several years before. Each week she led her class in a discussion of Scripture, prayed for them, and encouraged their spiritual development.

I also vaguely recalled she'd had a difficult marriage.

"My mom and dad divorced a few years ago," June continued. "Now Mom is bitter against God and other Christians. She's turned her back on the Lord and is into all sorts of New Age teachings."

"I'm so sorry," I said softly. "It must be very painful for you to see your mother reject everything she raised you to believe."

Our conversation clung to my mind. *Why did June's mother turn away?* I questioned. *Was she really committed to the Lord? Had she come into a life-changing relationship with Him? Or did she only have a surface experience of God—going to church and serving in various ways but without a living faith? Was her involvement prompted by religious feelings or genuine belief?*

Further questions tumbled through my mind: *How much Bible knowledge did she have? Was she aware that Jesus warned, "In this world you will have trouble"? Did she know He never said everything would always be rosy? Just how deep was her foundation in Jesus Christ that when trouble came she failed to stand?*

I didn't know the answers to these questions, but God does. My thoughts turned inward. *What about me?* I pondered. *If I had experienced the same storms in my life, would I still be standing?*

None of us escapes life's storms—ordinary or extraordinary human suffering. Whether it's the stabbing pain of a broken marriage, the heartache caused by a rebellious child, the terror of a debilitating disease, or any number of painful trials, few of us go through life without tears and sorrow. Nor do we always receive advance notice that a crisis is about to envelop us.

One of my favorite old hymns asks, "Shall I be carried to the skies on flowery beds of ease, while others fought to win the prize and sailed through bloody seas?" Every time I sing this line, my mind conjures up images of a California Rose Bowl Parade, where beautiful princesses recline on beds of roses and languidly wave at the crowds.

What's my response to the question, "Shall I be carried to the skies on flowery beds of ease?" An overwhelming, "Yes, Yes! That's exactly what I want." After all, who wouldn't choose to float through life on flowery beds of ease, until finally we are carried gently to be with the Lord? Who wants to battle bloody seas? Wouldn't you rather be surrounded by rose petals than thorns? I know I would!

Be honest. Don't you wish God provided Christians with invisible armor so the arrows of life would simply bounce off? Wouldn't it be wonderful if He had issued us supernatural parachutes so we could bail out whenever life gets tough? Or given us our own private cloud of blessings to float about on, a place immune from suffering?

Well, enough dreaming. The truth is, we *are* God's dearly loved children, but that doesn't insulate us from life's storms. Jesus wasn't one to soft-pedal the truth. He spelled it out clearly: "In this world you will have trouble." But knowing how quickly we feel overwhelmed by troubles, He immediately added a triumphant reminder: "Take heart! I have overcome the world" (John 16:33).

No matter what we're called to go through individually, God promises to be with us. He won't necessarily remove us from our trials, but promises to always go through them with us, giving us what we need to survive if not thrive. The question we need to ask, then, isn't "*Will* I face life's storms?" but rather "*How* can I stay standing in life's storms?" In our quest for growth, how can we come out stronger, more deeply rooted in Christ?

To discover answers that will keep us from collapsing in a heap of cynical rage, we need to explore four underlying questions:

• Why do storms come?

• What is God's purpose?

• What difference does my perspective make?

• How can I cope?

Why Do Storms Come?

"I'm so sorry," the doctor murmured to Janet soon after she'd delivered her second child, a baby girl. "Your baby has some serious problems."

As the weeks unfolded, Janet walked through a living nightmare as Claire, her little girl, struggled to live. "The tests show Claire is blind and severely retarded," Janet choked out. "She can't suckle, she has a malformed brain, and the doctors don't expect her to live more than a few years—and then, only if she's fed by a tube inserted into her stomach."

Questions wrack us when we suffer. *Why do storms slam into our lives, leaving us devastated and broken? Why is there suffering and evil? What have we done to deserve this? Is God so powerless or so uncaring He can't stop human suffering?* We struggle with these same questions when we share in the heartache of others.

As Christians, our resources to both survive and grow spiritually stronger come through our relationship with God, based on insights from Scripture. God and His Word is the answer to our questions, our help amid confusion, and our comfort in pain.

Referring to the Bible, John Stott states, "Although there are references to sin and suffering on virtually every page, its concern is not to explain their origin but to help us to overcome them."[1] Even though we can't be privy to mysteries known only to God, let's see what we can learn to help us stand in life's storms.

Suffering was not in God's original plan. Everything God made was given His stamp of approval. "God saw all that he had made, and it was very good" (Genesis 1:31). It was never His plan that humankind suffer the pain and brokenness we see around us and in our own lives. God's plan was that His creation fellowship perfectly with Him and enjoy His absolute goodness. Because of Satan, all this was marred, leaving us to suffer sin's consequences daily.

Scripture lets us glimpse Satan's activity. For example: Job's experience showed Satan as the source of his suffering; Jesus described a woman as "bound by Satan"; and Paul referred to his "thorn in the flesh" as a "messenger of Satan." Clearly, suffering is linked to Satan's activity in this world—a world that God created for our enjoyment.

Suffering often comes through people's choices. A drunk driver crashes into a teenager headed to the prom. A jealous spouse lashes out verbally and physically at his terrified wife. An angry mother loses control and beats her child. Much of the pain, sorrow, and heartbreak all around us is a result of human choices. Whenever people make choices without considering their devastating effects on others, someone suffers.

On a larger scale, look behind wars, famines, and many ecological disasters. The same cause becomes apparent. Without regard for the harm done to others, human greed, ambition, and callousness wreck lives on a personal and global scale. Ironically, God is blamed for what we human beings choose to do with our God-given freedom.

Suffering comes from sensitivity to pain. Don't you wish God had made us without the ability to feel physical pain? Some people do have this ability, but they don't consider it a blessing. Because they lack sensitivity to pain, leprosy sufferers can't tell if their hands have been burned, their feet cut, or their tongues chewed into ribbons.

Leprosy specialist Dr. Paul Brand pioneered rehabilitation work in India among those afflicted with what is now called Hanson's disease. Horrified by the effects of a body without pain receptors, he marveled at God's wisdom in designing a system that warns us of danger. Much as we dread it, pain is necessary for us to live as healthy a life as possible.

Although God is not the originator of sin and human suffering, nevertheless, He uses it as a tool to accomplish His purposes. Janet's little girl, Claire, died shortly after her second birthday. At the memorial service, Janet read several entries from her diary. Addressing teary-eyed friends, she said, "God has changed my heart and my attitudes over the past two years. I was angry and bitter toward Him; I felt cheated of a normal little girl, and I was embarrassed by Claire's appearance. But now I thank God for His love and help; I couldn't have survived without Him. Most of all, I thank Him for filling me with love for Claire. I will miss her so much." Yes, the howling storm did swallow up two years of Janet's life, but God used it to change her for eternity.

In God's hands, no suffering experienced by His children is either meaningless or endless. When He allows us to go through difficult times, He has a purpose, an end product in mind. Let's explore what some of these are.

What Is God's Purpose?

Several years ago I came across four questions I find helpful to ask not only in howling storms but also when life takes unexpected turns. Proverbs states, "Blessed is the man who finds wisdom, the man who gains understanding" (3:13). By turning these four questions into prayers, we open ourselves up to wisdom, insight that only God can give. Rather than wasting our tough experiences, let's prayerfully probe for God's purposes and the growth He intends for us. Here are the questions to ask:

* What does God want to do in this?

* What does God want to produce in me through this?

* What does God want to reveal about himself to me and through me?

* How does God want to use my trial to benefit others?

What does God want to do in this?

"Poppy, would you pray about becoming the class administrator?" inquired Judy, the teaching leader of the Bible study class I attended. Shortly after God had zeroed in on my jealous attitude toward Denise, Judy had invited me to become a discussion leader. Naturally, I jumped at the opportunity. Now, four months later, she asked me to become her assistant.

Loathe to leave my class of eager young women, I struggled with God, telling Him I didn't like His change of plans one bit. After all, I had just begun this new adventure. I was a raw recruit. After a weekend of resisting, I submitted, sensing this new direction was from Him. A few years later, when I was asked to take Judy's position, I saw why He put me in that place of learning and growth.

Think of something you're facing right now, or have faced. Now begin prayerfully asking God, "What do You want to do in this

150

situation? Do You want to change my direction? To deepen my faith? To mold me for something You are planning at a future time? Have You allowed this situation to come crashing into my life because You have a greater design than I can see right now? Lord, help me trust You and cooperate with Your purposes in this situation."

In our finite human wisdom, there are many times when we can find no reason at all for what God has allowed. When this happens, remember Joseph. He couldn't possibly understand what God was doing when his brothers sold him into slavery, his employer's wife falsely accused him, and his so-called friend forgot about him in prison. But in God's timing, he recognized there was a divine purpose behind all he had endured. With God-given insight, he could say to his cringing brothers, "You intended to harm me, but God intended it for good" (Genesis 50:20).

We might not know what God is doing, but we can respond rightly in the situation—and be confident God has a purpose in allowing it. Think about something tough you are facing right now and write down any insights that come to you as you consider the question "What does God want to do in this situation?"

What does God want to produce in me through this?

"I prided myself on doing everything well," Yvonne confessed. "I was a perfectionist and I know I came across rather hard at times. If I felt someone didn't quite measure up to my standard, I didn't show them much compassion or understanding.

"Then came my emotional breakdown, which was a shattering experience for me, as it is for anyone. But God used it in my life. He not only drew me closer to Him, He also broke my hard attitudes toward other people. Instead of my old 'I can do this perfectly' attitude, I find myself asking God to work through me as I depend on Him."

Yvonne's tenderness toward others is apparent now, leading many women to seek her input and wisdom. And because of what God allowed, even the most difficult and most needy people He brings across Yvonne's path find her a warm and understanding friend. In God's hands, she emerged from the storm more like the Lord than ever before.

As you look at your own stormy experiences, prayerfully ask God, "What do You want to produce in me through the experience I'm facing now? Could it be a yieldedness to Your will rather than my own? Sensitivity to others? Trust in You? Courage to act and not hold back from what You are asking me to do? Are You wanting me to draw closer, to learn to lean on You through this storm? To move from my stagnant faith to one that is alive and growing?"

What do you sense God wants to produce in you?

What does God want to reveal about himself to me and through me?

"I was sitting at the kitchen table reading my Bible the other day," said Pam, "and had put a Christian tape on. It was playing softly in the background, but suddenly I found myself listening to the words: 'I am the God that healeth thee, I am the Lord, your healer.'

"As I thought of how God had turned my marriage around and removed the bitterness I felt for so many years, I was overwhelmed. I started crying and praying at the same time as I realized that the Lord had been my healer."

Pam felt she had made a terrible mistake after only six months of marriage. She and her husband, Tom, had different opinions on almost everything—from musical tastes to dealing with conflict. They clashed constantly. Three years later the tension between them led Pam to feel divorce was the only solution. As the only Christian in her family, however, Pam wrestled with the impact a divorce would make on her witness to them. She could imagine them saying, "I thought being a Christian made a difference in how people solved their problems. It doesn't seem to have helped you." She also searched the Bible to see if there were biblical grounds for divorce. But incompatibility wasn't one of them. Finally, she begged God to let her walk away. Instead, she sensed Him impressing on her mind the words *Divorce is not the answer.*

"I decided not to get a divorce," Pam continued. "In fact, I made a conscious choice to stay in my marriage and turn to God with all the pain I felt. So when I listened to the song 'You Are the Lord, My Healer,' I couldn't help looking back over the past twenty years and thanking God for what He had done. Through the years I have felt loved and accepted by Him. I know it seems strange to say this, because I'm far from perfect, but I feel His delight in me."

What did God reveal of himself to Pam? She experienced God as her Strength and Sustainer, as well as her Healer. Pam also recognized that God, in His divine wisdom, had used a seemingly hopeless marriage as a school for spiritual growth for both her and Tom.

What does God want to reveal to you about himself? Could He want to show you that He is faithful and will supply the strength you need? That He is wise and all-knowing—the One you can rely on? Does He want to reveal himself as your Healer—from hurt, pain, abuse, a great loss in your life? Could He be allowing a situation so you will turn to Him and deal with an area that needs attention?

The psalmist declares God is "a shield around me ... my strength ... my rock, my fortress and my deliverer ... my light and my salvation ... the stronghold of my life" (3:3; 18:1-2; 27:1). He is also a source of joy when we're in the midst of a joyless situation. These are all attributes and characteristics of God that He wants to reveal to us when we're in difficult situations.

What aspect of His character is becoming real to you in your difficult place?

How does God want to use my trial to benefit others?

"Of course I want to live to see my girls grow up," said Amy, "but if the cancer takes me before that happens, the most important thing will be seeing the three of them put their faith in Christ."

Amy's trust in God's sovereign wisdom shone through the three years she battled breast cancer. Being human, she prayed for healing and longed to have life return to normal—but it didn't happen. Instead, God used her trial to inspire many Christian friends to be more serious about their own walk with God and witnessing to others. One by one, her three girls came to put their faith in Christ. Their mother's prayers throughout her trial brought them eternal benefit.

Paul praised God as the "Father of compassion and the God of all comfort, who comforts *us* in all our troubles, so that *we* can comfort those in any trouble with the comfort we ourselves have received from God" (2 Corinthians 1:3-4). When God allows us to go through trials, He intends others to benefit also.

In the right place, at the right time, and in an appropriate way, sharing the storms in our lives might be God's lifeline to another hurting person. Let's ask God, "How do You want to use my trial to benefit others?" Then watch for His direction. As we make ourselves available to encourage others, we can help them stand in life's storms. Take a moment to reflect on ways your trial might benefit others. Write down what God is saying to you.

Wringing good out of evil and growth out of pain is God's specialty. Scripture illustrates this and so do the true-life stories given in this chapter. God doesn't shield us from the pain that comes with living in a fallen world, but He uses it to accomplish His loving purposes.

We choose which perspective to take when God allows life's storms to slam into us. We can bitterly fight against His ways, or accept that in His love and wisdom He has permitted it for our good. What difference does your perspective make? The difference between running away and staying put, falling apart and standing strong.

What Difference Does My Perspective Make?

A story is told about a unique garage sale. One day Satan decided to put all his tools out for sale. He laid out malice, gossip, jealousy, pride, lying, lust, and everything else he carried in his bag of tricks. All of the tools were priced for a quick sale—except for one.

A buyer sauntered around eyeing the different tools and appreciating the prices. But when he saw that one was priced many times higher than the others, he paused. Going over to Satan he asked, "Why is this tool priced so much higher than any of the others?"

With a sly smile Satan responded, "Because this is my most effective tool, the one I use constantly."

Do you know what it was? *Discouragement!*

Discouragement whispers, "Give up. It's hopeless. Why keep trying?" When our perspective is "God has abandoned me. He doesn't care. He has no power. He is not good," we go down like a tree uprooted by the wind.

Part of our task in pursuing maturity is learning to fight back against our completely human yet spiritually destructive reactions. To keep standing, our perspective has to be formed by Scripture. However, knowledge of what God says isn't enough. We have to embrace biblical truth by faith, letting it change our thinking and response to trials. With this in mind, let's look at two crucial Scriptures to help us rearrange how we think about trials: Romans 8:28 and James 1:2-4.

Romans 8:28

> And we know that in all things God works for the good of those who love him, who have been called according to his purpose.

Paul doesn't say that everything that happens to us is good. Some things are most definitely not, and God doesn't tell us to delude ourselves or call evil good. What Paul does declare is that God works all the events in our lives—awful or awesome—together for our benefit.

What makes it possible for all things to work together for our ultimate good? Dr. Vernon Grounds, former president of Conservative Baptist Seminary in Colorado, states, "The answer is simple. God is at work in the whole process! And by His infinite power and love God is making all things work together for good."[2] He is weaving the individual events of our lives into something beautiful, which we cannot possibly see when trying to make sense of the individual parts.

We might well question, "How can what has happened to me, or to someone I love, turn out for good?" But "good" as defined by us and "good" as defined by God are as different as we are from God! He is looking at His eternal purposes for us;

we are looking at our earthly pleasure, comfort, and satisfaction. "When at last we bear perfectly the likeness of Jesus, we will confess that the logic of divine love was infinitely above and beyond our human logic. To be like Jesus, we will understand eventually, is the only true and abiding good."[3]

To stay standing, our perspective of what's happening has to be formed by faith in the promise that God *is* working all things together for our good. We might not see it in our lifetime, but we will see it in eternity.

James 1:2-4

> Consider it pure joy ... whenever you face trials of many
> kinds, because you know that the testing of your faith
> develops perseverance. Perseverance must finish its work
> so that you may be mature and complete, not lacking
> anything.

James takes our breath away with his forthright statement that we
should consider it pure joy to face trials. Is he living in a different
world? Or does he have a perspective we can learn from? Notice
he says trials of every variety are tests of our faith. Whenever we
face them, we have the opportunity to prove that we really believe
in God and trust Him with our lives.

The greatest testing of my faith came when I arrived in America as
a newly married twenty-two-year-old. I had said "I do" to a man
from a country and culture I had never visited and whose
background, I soon discovered, was as opposite from mine as the
North and South Poles. Was this a tough way to begin married
life? Yes! In the years of struggling to adjust, I remember reading
James's confident words, "For you know that the testing of your
faith develops perseverance." The problem was, I didn't know. I
didn't have a clue why God had allowed my life to become one
challenge after another.

Perhaps you've felt the same way. It wasn't until several years
later that I understood God was at work in the situation to make me
like Christ. Grasping this truth didn't cause the challenges to
disappear, but knowing God had a purpose in it all provided both
comfort and motivation to persevere. In order to stand, we have to
know, deep within our being, that God is working in us for our
good—that through trials, He is developing perseverance, a stick-
to-it-iveness that is vital to a mature faith. Unaware of this truth, it
is hard to persevere, let alone consider trials a joy because they
develop our faith in God.

Perseverance obviously implies a length of time. After all, who perseveres for two minutes? Or two days? We can't possibly endure for a brief moment and then emerge with a mature faith. No, James says, perseverance must finish its work. Whatever God is producing in us takes time—how long is known only to God. When the trial goes on and on, it's easy to think we've been forgotten or forsaken, but we haven't been. God is still at work, using the circumstances to produce the qualities He wants to shine through us.

Some of life's storms are brief and violent. Others engulf our lives like a stalled hurricane. Whichever storm has touched you, let your perspective be formed by the truth that God intends trials to bring you closer to the maturity of Christ. It's been said, "God is too kind to do anything cruel, and too wise ever to make a mistake." If this affirmation of God's character forms your perspective, you will stand.

How Can I Cope?

An atheist who was ill and bedridden had two sons. Determined to sway them to his way of thinking, he asked the younger one to write on a chalkboard beside his bed the words "God is nowhere." Later, when his older son came into his bedroom he asked him to read what was written on the board. In a strong voice, the boy read, "God is now here."

When storms barrel into us, our first reaction might well be "God is nowhere." But when we understand God works in every storm for our good and His glory, the truth that "God is now here" rescues us from panic and collapse.

In 1991 a head-on car crash took the lives of Gerald Sittser's mother, wife, and four-year-old daughter. He writes of his thoughts immediately after receiving news of the tragedy: "I realized I would have to suffer and adjust; I could not avoid it or escape it. There was no way but ahead, into the abyss.... I faced the test of my life. One phase of my life had ended; another, the most difficult, was about to begin."

Later, he wrote of living with his overwhelming grief: "I did not go through pain and come out the other side; instead, I lived in it and found within that pain the grace to survive and eventually grow."[4]

How can we survive and grow in the storms that swirl into our lives? Listen to what Jesus says: "Everyone who hears these words of mine and *puts them into practice* is like a wise man who built his house on the rock. The rain came down, the streams rose, and the winds blew and beat against that house; yet it did not fall, because it had its foundation upon the rock. But everyone who hears these words of mine and *does not put them into practice* is like a foolish man who built his house on sand. The rains came down, the streams rose, and the winds blew and beat against that house, and it fell with a great crash" (Matthew 7:24-27, emphasis added).

The resources to cope, to stay standing in our storms, are available to us. By putting into practice what God has revealed to us, we can come through spiritually stronger than we were. Stunningly painful as they might be, storms don't have to knock us off our feet, throwing us into a cynical bitterness toward God. Jesus promised that if we put His words into practice, we will stand. Let's see how Scripture instructs us to do this.

1. *Cling to God's character.* Crying out "Why?" and doubting God's love might well be our first reaction to painful circumstances. And Scripture—particularly the Psalms—shows many a loud and long "*Why*, God?" But as Christians we move on from there. Scripture clearly reveals that our Father is a God of love, compassion, and wisdom. Peter teaches this, saying, "Cast all your anxiety on him because he cares for you" (1 Peter 5:7). John proclaims, "How great is the love the Father has lavished on us, that we should be called children of God!" (1 John 3:1). The

prophet Habakkuk, facing the destruction of his people and the devastation of their land, said of God, "The Sovereign Lord is my strength; he makes my feet like the feet of a deer, he enables me to go on the heights" (Habakkuk 3:19).

These are the truths we must search out in our Bibles, rehearse in our minds, and choose to believe despite our circumstances. If we keep our hearts firmly fixed on God's proven character, declaring to Him, "No matter what happens, You are the Sovereign Lord and I will walk with You," He will enable us to stand.

2. *Consider Christ's sufferings.* Our Enemy loves to hear us accuse God of being indifferent to our suffering. Even better is when we imagine God seated in heaven, His arms crossed, harshly saying, "Stop sniveling." When these blasphemous ideas spill into our minds, we need to smack them back to where they came from.

When we're weary and losing heart, the writer of Hebrews points us to Jesus: "Let us fix our eyes on Jesus.... Consider him who endured...." (12:2-3). Picture Jesus on the cross, arms out-stretched, and you will see the extent of God's love.

"But," we might protest in our misery, "does God know what human suffering is like?" Again, look at Jesus, wracked with pain, unable to move his limbs, rejected and despised. He was no stranger to suffering, either emotional or physical, and He bears the wounds of Calvary to this day. If God didn't love us, would He have allowed His Son to suffer like this?

3. *Call for God's help.* One of the most powerful coping tools given to Christians is the privilege of praying to a caring and all-powerful heavenly Father. Hebrews 4:16 urges, "Let us then approach the throne of grace with confidence, so that we may receive mercy and find grace to help us in our time of need." Because we are accepted through Christ's death for us and adopted into God's family, God never grows weary of our coming to Him.

When given a "thorn in the flesh," a source of great pain, Paul responded as we would—praying persistently for deliverance. Instead of God removing his thorn, however, Paul received supernatural strength to carry on even while the thorn remained.

Like Paul, sometimes God's answer to a specific prayer is no or "not now." This is never easy, but trusting in God's wisdom and goodness does enable us to say, even through tears, "Not my will but Thine be done." Some situations, however, call for more than prayer. In order to cope, we must also take action. If you're in a destructive situation, pray about what to do, read the Word, seek the counsel of mature Christians, then take the steps God shows you.

Take every concern to God, appeal to Him for comfort, courage, and clear thinking. Keep drawing on His grace in your moment of need; pray always in all circumstances. God's promise to Paul is His promise to us: "My grace *is* sufficient for you, for my power is made perfect in weakness" (2 Corinthians 12:9).

4. *Claim God's promises to work for good.* In the middle of a trial it is often hard to see what good can come of it. But remember, we're called to walk by faith, to look at the unseen rather than the seen, to affirm what Scripture declares: "God is at work for good."

Feed your faith on promises from the Word, starting with these strong affirmations: " 'For I know the plans I have for you,' declares the Lord, 'plans to prosper you and not to harm you, plans to give you hope and a future. When you pass through the waters, I will be with you; and when you pass through the rivers, they will not sweep over you. When you walk through the fire, you will not be burned; the flames will not set you ablaze. For I am the Lord, your God, the Holy One of Israel, your Savior....' And the God of all grace, who called you to his eternal glory in Christ, after you have suffered a little while, will himself restore you and make you strong, firm and steadfast" (Jeremiah 29:11; Isaiah 43:2-3; 1 Peter 5:10).

As the storm swirls around you, be alert to the little blessings, the encouraging "coincidences," the whispers of assurance given to your heart by the Holy Spirit. Thank God, by faith, for the good that will come from your trial—then begin looking for it.

5. *Conquer worry.* "Do not worry about your life.... Do not worry about tomorrow," said Jesus (Matthew 6:25-34). Expanding on Jesus' words, Paul commands, "Do not be anxious about anything, but in everything, by prayer and petition, with thanksgiving, present your requests to God" (Philippians 4:6). And what is the promised result? Inward peace, calm, and freedom from worry, not only when our storms are over but in the middle of them.

"Now wait a minute," we respond. "This is ridiculous. How on earth can we go through tough places without worrying? Can anyone live like this in the real world?" We might find it hard to imagine ourselves reaching this spiritual pinnacle, but *Christians are never told to aim for something that isn't possible through God's power.*

Conquering worry begins with prayer, acknowledging that in ourselves we can't overcome this automatic response to life. The next step is to ask ourselves some blunt questions: "What am I worried about? Is worrying helping me or making me feel more tense and upset? How do I know if my worries will come true?" In addition to questioning ourselves, we need to confess to God that we're not trusting Him, ask His forgiveness, and reaffirm our confidence in His ability to care for us.

None of us knows what tomorrow holds. So why lose today's peace to what might never happen? *And if our worst fears should come true, God has promised He will supply what we need at that time—but not before.* When we anxiously chew things over, we're taking on concerns that God has told us to give to Him. Hard as it is to break the old patterns, new ways of dealing with our worries can be developed. A good beginning place is to memorize David's statement, "When I am afraid, I will trust in you. In God, whose word I praise, in God I trust; I will not be afraid" (Psalm 56:3-4). Then, every time anxious thoughts pop into your mind, deliberately hand them over to God.

6. *Cultivate your friendships.* Don't hibernate in your heartache. Let people care for you physically, emotionally, and spiritually. Christians are to "carry each other's burdens" (Galatians 6:2). Hiding behind a facade of "I'm fine" when we're falling apart cuts us off from help God sends through others in the body of Christ. Let yourself be real. Allow yourself to be loved and ministered to.

Not only does Scripture tell us to care for one another, medical research shows the benefits of giving and receiving support. "Confiding in someone may offer big payoffs in terms of health," say experts from Stanford University School of Medicine who compared two groups of women with breast cancer. They found that those who attended support meetings had lower levels of pain, less stress and depression, and their survival rates were nearly twice as high as the women who toughed it out on their own.[5]

In any trial, survival is more likely when others stand beside us. A friend's strength lifts us up when we're about to sink, her faith challenges us to trust when we're overwhelmed with doubts, and her continuous concern for our well-being assures us we're not forgotten. God doesn't call us to go through our darkest days with an "it's just God and me" attitude. Opening the door to spiritually mature friends to walk beside us is God's idea. He knows we need the support of others to help us emerge from our trials strong and more rooted in our faith. So let's grab hold of those outstretched hands He has brought to us, thanking Him for His provision to stay standing.

Going through life's storms is never easy, but God knows what He is doing. Using all the circumstances we encounter, He is at work painstakingly transforming us into the likeness of His Son. For this to happen, He must deepen our faith and lead us into a greater level of trust. Will we permit Him to accomplish His purposes?

"All the Way My Savior Leads Me"

> All the way my Savior leads me,
>
> what have I to ask beside?
>
> Can I doubt His faithful mercies,
>
> who thru life has been my Guide?
>
> Heavenly peace, divinest comfort,
>
> here by faith in Him to dwell!
>
> For I know what e'er befalls me,
>
> Jesus doeth all things well.
>
> All the way my Savior leads me,
>
> cheers each winding path I tread,
>
> gives me strength for ev'ry trial,
>
> feeds me with the living bread.
>
> Tho my weary steps may falter
>
> and my soul athirst may be,
>
> gushing from the Rock before me,
>
> Lo! A spring of joy I see.
>
> —Fanny Crosby

Reflections—for Thought and Discussion

1. What major storm have you faced in your life? How did you come through it?

2. Describe your initial response to a crisis situation—what do you feel; what do you think; how do you act; what are your thoughts about God?

3. What help or fresh insights did you find in the section *Why Do Storms Come*?

4. When have you looked back on a situation and felt you understood something of God's purposes in allowing it? What was your response to this insight?

5. What qualities or positive changes has God produced in you through a difficult time in your life?

6. How has God become more precious to you as a result of going through a storm?

7. Read and reflect on the Scriptures found in the section *How Can I Cope*? Which of these principles have helped you in a time of need? Is there someone you might lovingly share these with this week?

Memory Verse

"We fix our eyes not on what is seen, but on what is unseen. For what is seen is temporary, but what is unseen is eternal" (2 Corinthians 4:18).

Notes:

1 John Stott, *The Cross of Christ* (Leicester, England: InterVarsity Press, 1986), 312.

2 Vernon Grounds, "Do All Things Really Work Together for Good?" (seminary handout).

3 Ibid.

4 Gerald Sittser, *A Grace Disguised: How the Soul Grows Through Loss* (Grand Rapids, Mich.: Zondervan Publishing House, 1997).

5 Rebecca Stowe, "Friends as Healers," *Modern Maturity* (Sept.-Oct. 1997).

NINE

Can My Stumbling Blocks Become Stepping Stones?

SOME PEOPLE STRIDE THROUGH LIFE WITHOUT SEEMING TO stumble over anything—at least not in front of others. Then there are the rest of us. Whether it's falling off a bike onto lava rocks before I'd even begun to pedal, or tripping over a kitchen rug while clutching bags of groceries and breaking my arm, when it comes to anything remotely physical, I'm a stumbler.

Perhaps you're different. You might be one of those smooth and elegant women who glides through a room or has mastered the art of looking classy while climbing out of a van. Maybe you've never tripped over anything in public, got your foot stuck in a car while the rest of your body is half-in and half-out—or had to disentangle yourself, Houdini-like, from your handbag straps, which mysteriously knotted themselves around your seat belt.

Whether we're klutzy or classy, however, there is one area of life that causes all of us to stumble. It's called *temptation.*

Eve, eyeing the fruit in the Garden, wanted what God said was "off-limits." She was tempted—which is not a sin. Her failure came when she disobeyed God's clear command, choosing to determine for herself right from wrong. With one bite of the forbidden fruit, she tumbled from temptation into sin. And every one of us has followed in her footsteps.

Which of us hasn't heard subtle whispers or loud demands urging, "Eat me" when we spy luscious, junky food we've vowed to avoid, "Buy me" when we're trying to quit running up more debt, or "Look at me" as we struggle to maintain a pure mind in an impure world? Who hasn't been tempted to shout or accuse, refuse to

167

apologize, look down on others, or ignore a need they could meet? Temptations come in myriad shapes and sizes. Whatever form they take, their pull is powerful.

Like fish confronted by an eye-catching lure, we often swim around the temptation pondering what to do. "Should I or shouldn't I?" we debate, rather than moving away as rapidly as we can. Then, overwhelmed by desire for what promises to bring instant satisfaction, we bite. "After all," we reason, "how can I resist what must be right because it feels so good?" Chomping on the bait, we're caught. Chalk up one more victory for Satan.

None of us swims through life without coming face-to-face with temptation. At some point, we've all swallowed the bait. Our old nature has programmed us to want whatever we find appealing to our senses, whether God has said it's off-limits or not. Should we just accept, then, that failure to resist temptation is inevitable? Understandable? Even acceptable, given our backgrounds, circumstances, or temperament? Is true change impossible? Are thoughts of overcoming instead of succumbing just dreamy delusions? Is hiding in shame from God and living with a permanent whiff of guilt in our nostrils the only way to cope with repeated failure?

God's answer is a resounding "NO!" Although all of us have fought and failed time and again to overcome a recurring sin, such a defeatist mentality should have no place in our lives.

By definition, we are "Christ's ones," members of His family, with unlimited access to His resources to overcome our weaknesses. Help is available for stumbling humans like us. But let's remember, no quick fixes exist. Change comes as we turn to the Holy Spirit with our weaknesses and cooperate with His directions. He helps us develop new response patterns. However, as with any deeply entrenched reaction, this takes time and discipline, plus knowledge of the "how to's."

In order to check how much you know about temptation, try taking this quick quiz—then look for the answers as we explore the ways our stumbling blocks can become stepping stones to a closer relationship with God. Don't worry if your score is zero; it simply means you'll learn more about how to grow, which is what we're aiming for.

Do you know any of the wonderfully encouraging promises of God regarding temptation? If so, write one down as best you remember it.

Are you aware of your own weaknesses? Write down one or two areas where you experience temptation.

Do you know what triggers these vulnerable areas in you? What are they?

Are you aware of what needs to be ejected from your life in order to make progress in resisting Satan's bait? Put down what comes to mind.

Do you know what action you need to take in order to grow stronger when tempted?

Now that we've put ourselves in the picture, let's learn how to replace old patterns with new ones. Here are three helpful steps:

1. Face the facts about temptation.

2. Trace your personal trouble spots.

3. Embrace God's ways of escape.

Face the Facts About Temptation

Have you ever thought, *I'm a terrible failure as a Christian. No one else stumbles the way I do. I'll never be strong enough to resist this temptation?* Probably most of us have. But are these thoughts accurate? Notice the following statements about temptation and then check your facts again.

"No temptation has seized you except what is common to man [and woman]. And God is faithful; he will not let you be tempted beyond what you can bear. But when you are tempted, he will also provide a way out so that you can stand up under it" (1 Corinthians 10:13). Wow! Look at the understanding and hope packed into this one verse. Don't you find it chock-full of encouragement for all of us who stumble yet long to grow strong in Christ? We dare not miss what this verse is saying.

Temptation Is Common to All

Walking out of a children's clothing store with my then five-year-old son, Elliot, I noticed him clutching something in his little fist. "What do you have in your hand, Elliot?" I asked. Uncurling his fingers, he said nothing as I looked at the plastic ring with its fake blue stone.

"Did you take that from the store?" I asked. He nodded. Needless to say, we talked about what he'd done, then returned the ring to the shop, where he apologized for taking it.

Temptation doesn't stop when we reach the wise old age of, say, six. It surrounds us whether we're five, six, sixteen, or thirty-six. We see, we want, we take, determining for ourselves what is right or wrong. The apostle James writes, "Each one is tempted when, by his own evil desire, he is dragged away and enticed" (1:14).

Stimulation to sin comes not only from our inner desires but also through messages beamed into our souls by the world we live in. And lurking behind everything that entices us from both within and without is our great enemy, Satan himself.

Temptation is a part of everyone's life. You and I are not terrible monsters because we struggle with our flaws and failings—we are normal human beings, responsive to urgings to sin. But we are also far more than that. We are new creatures in Christ, possessors of new hearts, no longer puppets who must sin when our strings are pulled. We don't *have* to stumble over and over.

Hear this and have hope—God says He controls our temptations. He promises they will never be more than we can bear.

Temptation Is Controlled by God

Does God tempt us to do evil? "No," says James emphatically (1:13). "God is light; in him there is no darkness at all" (1 John 1:5). God is holy, totally separate from sin. He can never prompt us to do what He hates.

Does He, then, shield us from circumstances that tempt us to sin? No again. To accomplish this, God would have to take us from earth to heaven the moment we put our faith in Christ. In previous centuries, men and women who longed to be holy separated themselves from society, believing this would shield them from temptation. But what happened? They discovered that as long as they were in the body, they could never be entirely free of temptation. Jesus' accurate summary of the source of temptation had been forgotten: "*out of the heart* come evil thoughts, murder, adultery, sexual immorality, theft, false testimony, slander" (Matthew 15:19, emphasis mine).

God never tempts us to do evil, nor does He shield us from tempting circumstances. Strangely, He does permit us to be tempted—for a good purpose. Consider these three reasons:

1. Temptation tests and reveals who we love the most, whose will we will follow, who is No. 1 in our lives. Is it ourselves, our wants, our rights, or is it God?

2. Temptation shows us how much of our old nature still lurks within, needing the changing work of the Holy Spirit.

3. Temptation gives us an opportunity to experience God's mercy and kindness in action, as He provides a way for us to resist.

God promises we will never face a temptation we cannot resist—whether it's giving in to anger, evil desires, or any other powerful pull of our flesh or the world. If we do disobey and give in, we can't blame God or anyone else.

When we're under the hypnotic power of temptation, let's remember, God is in control of both its duration and depth. He will never permit the temptation to be more overwhelming than the resources He provides. He will provide a way out. He will enable us to stand. But we are responsible to reach out and take hold of the resources to do so.

Temptation Is Conquerable With God's Aid

If you saw a truck barreling down the road toward you, would you stand and stare at it without getting out of the way? Of course not! In similar fashion, if we know we're in spiritual danger of being knocked down and splattered all over the landscape, doesn't it make sense to run in the opposite direction?

Remember Joseph, whose masculine charms tempted Potiphar's wife until she tried to seduce him? As an obedient servant he couldn't stay out of her presence, but he conquered the temptation to sin by living in the presence of Someone Else. Notice what gave him the power to resist: "My master has withheld nothing from me except you, because you are his wife. How then could I do such a wicked thing and *sin against God*?" To Joseph, God's approval meant more than any brief, illicit pleasure.

To experience God's power to escape or bear up under a temptation, we must genuinely want it. But isn't it all too true to say that sometimes we want to escape—and sometimes we don't?

Taking hold of God's promised power is essentially a matter of the heart. Do we secretly enjoy the sin that so easily trips us up? Does it give us a sense of power or satisfaction? Or do we sincerely long for victory and grieve over our failures? These issues must be faced with searing honesty. Until we ache for change, we won't look for, or taste, God's delivering power.

Take a moment to reflect honestly on your feelings regarding a besetting sin in your life—then write a prayer telling God what your heart desires the most.

Trace Your Personal Trouble Spots

"God," I wept in frustration, "how can I ever control my temper? I lose it with Jim and the kids before I even know I'm angry. You've got to help me or I'll never change."

With those words, God went to work on a stumbling block I constantly tripped over. Now, I can give many valid reasons for my problem, as you probably can for yours. For instance, parental modeling: My mother said whatever popped into her head if anyone in the family crossed her—and I often did the same.

Another reason is personal circumstances. For me, it was myriad: the stress of living in an unfamiliar culture; reluctantly attending a church dominated by unwritten rules regarding beliefs and lifestyle; having a husband who worked long hours; having no family nearby; little money; small children to care for alone. But regardless of contributing factors, the truth remains—I permitted my old nature to run free. My ability to fuss, fume, and blow my top—all in a split second—wracked me with feelings of misery, failure, and guilt. I felt helpless because I hadn't been aware of my getting angry or that a different response was possible, because provocation and reaction happened so fast. When the bait was waved in front of me, I swallowed it instantly, giving Satan constant victories in my life.

Some temptations come with lightning speed. Others increase in hypnotic power the longer we linger near them. Both have the power to trip us up. But whatever shape our particular temptations take, Scripture clearly states we are not helpless victims without the hope of change.

Part of foiling Satan's temptations to sin comes through tracing and acknowledging where we're particularly vulnerable and weak. Armed with this understanding of ourselves, we're more likely to spot what will trip us up *before rather than after the fact*.

Let's do some tracing.

The Power of the Past

My anger problem, though it was triggered by all the difficult changes in my life, had definite roots in the past. This doesn't excuse the sin involved, but explains why resisting that particular temptation had become such a severe struggle.

Sometimes our habitual stumbling blocks *are* linked to the past. We developed deeply rooted habit patterns, believed certain responses were normal, or were enmeshed in particular practices that we now know are sin. These stumbling blocks aren't removed automatically the moment you and I become Christians.

Look back, now, at the quiz questions. What did you note as areas where you most frequently experience temptation? Are they linked in any way to your past—either your upbringing and parental modeling or patterns of behavior you developed? Write down any connection you see.

Whenever our old responses persist, instead of despairing, let's recognize that God is able to use them as stepping stones to make us spiritually stronger. Through the Word and the promptings of the Holy Spirit, God teaches us how to overcome our old nature. He also provides the power to behave and think differently—as one of His children.

Becoming a Christian doesn't mean we're emotionally healed in an instant from the effects of our past. Nor are our emotions or thought processes made perfect when Christ indwells us. A work is going on in us; we're *being* built into the likeness of Christ. Becoming more like Him takes time, in fact, it takes a lifetime.

The Pressure of the Present

"Poppy, I've never told anyone about this, but I need help," said a woman who asked to talk to me privately after I'd spoken at a women's conference. "I've fallen in love with a man who dated my daughter. He's older than she is and from my country. We've been writing to each other for several months and have exchanged photos. My husband thinks of him as a friend and suspects nothing. I really want to please God, but I have longings for this man. What am I going to do?"

Not all temptations are linked to the past. Like the woman who sought me out, you may never have had a problem with lust before, but now your eye catches the warm, appreciative look of a male friend and the battle begins. Maybe you've never felt sorry for yourself in the past, but you've lost your job or a relationship has gone sour and you're tempted to wallow in self-pity. You've never been a critical, backbiting person, but now your rage at being betrayed by a friend tempts you to take revenge.

Ask yourself, "Does the temptation I'm struggling with have its source in a current situation? Or, if not, what did cause it?" Record your answer.

Probe for Clues

After praying for insight from the Lord as to what provoked my angry outbursts, I soon realized they were usually triggered by fear or frustration. In most cases, my anger surged when I felt helpless at not being able to control or even have a say in what was happening or might happen. I also recognized four stages that repeated themselves: impatience, frustration, an angry outburst, and depression. This is a cycle I still watch out for. When I find myself wrestling with any of these four stages, I begin probing for clues.

As you continue tracing your personal trouble spots, remember that God loves you unconditionally. Then prayerfully ask God to give you insight. We're instructed, "If any of you lacks wisdom, he [or she] should ask God" (James 1:5). Having done this, thoughtfully answer the following questions as you probe for hidden triggers in your life.

1. When does temptation come? What is the timing or circumstance?

2. Are there triggering events, words, or attitudes in myself or others that I recognize?

3. Are there places I go, people I spend time with, or ways I occupy myself that trigger temptation?

4. Why am I vulnerable to this? Is there some need, belief, or fear behind my response?

Stumbling blocks and what triggers them vary from person to person. What trips me up might not be a problem at all for you. What you find difficult to overcome might not trouble me. Regardless of our personal vulnerability to certain temptations, if we want to grow and mature, we all need to discover and embrace God's promised ways of escape.

Embrace God's Ways of Escape

Paul writes, "If you think you are standing firm, be careful that you don't fall!" (1 Corinthians 10:12). I know I'll always be vulnerable to angry words and outbursts given the right circumstances. But, there's something else I know: My old stumbling block that had the power to constantly trip me up, has become my ally. Here's how God helped me escape its grip. Perhaps some of what I learned will help you.

Anger: From Stumbling Block to Spiritual Stepping Stone

Following earnest prayer regarding this sin in my life, I began to sense when I was getting irritable. This had never happened before. Now, like a flashing road sign warning of trouble ahead, I immediately became alert to the direction I was headed. Then, as I continued to seek God's help, He impressed on me several definite steps to follow.

1. *Stop quarreling.* If I felt myself getting upset, the phrase "zip your lip" popped into my mind. I also took seriously the admonition "To quarrel with a neighbor is foolish; a man [woman] with good sense holds his [her] tongue" (Proverbs 11:12 TLB). If I found I couldn't hold my tongue (because I was so used to saying what was on it), then I took the next step. Leaving the room, I'd find a private place (usually the bathroom) and promptly dump all my feelings before the Lord—I figured if David could do it in the Psalms, so could I.

2. *Speak to God.* Pouring out my frustrations to God drained the adrenaline pumping through my veins. I knew enough to understand that this is a much healthier way to deal with anger than stewing in bitterness. I expressed what I felt to God, seeking His help to calm myself down. This was also much smarter than throwing around words that I could never take back.

3. *Seek His perspective.* I learned to pray, "Lord, help me with my attitudes and feelings. Show me why I'm reacting this way. Please give me insight." Sometimes what came to mind amazed me—that it was so petty, or that this was an innocent miscommunication. If I was still brooding angrily in the bathroom after praying for insight, I would then pray, "Lord, give me the desire to please You and a willing heart to confess my own sin in this situation." When I had done this, God directed me to take two more important steps.

4. *Seek reconciliation.* This involved both attitude and action. Knowing "all things work together for good," I chose to trust God

to do precisely that. In fact, I developed an attitude of expectancy and watched to see how He would work it for good. In pursuing reconciliation and healing, I began to pray for the person I was upset with (usually my poor husband), praising God for his good qualities. Then I looked for concrete ways to build bridges between us—including discussing the issue calmly at an appropriate time and apologizing where necessary.

5. *Seek wisdom.* I had no desire to go over the same ground again and again like a mini-brained hamster spinning around on its wheel. I wanted to change my behavior and attitudes. That meant acquiring some wisdom from God. Proverbs 18:15 says it well: "The heart of the discerning acquires knowledge; the ears of the wise seek it out." God intended for me to gain wisdom through His Word and prayer. But He also led me to seek help through books, tapes, sermons, and the confidential counsel of others who were more mature and knowledgeable.

We can rely on God's promise to be faithful, to provide a way out from giving in to temptation. Be encouraged—old response patterns can be broken. Our stumbling blocks can become stepping stones to a growing likeness to Jesus Christ.

Plan for Freedom

In *How to Say No to a Stubborn Habit*, pastor and author Erwin Lutzer writes, "He (God) uses your struggles to give you a thorough housecleaning, reorganize your priorities and make you dependent on His grace. There are no cheap, easy miracles. You must want spiritual freedom, not merely for your own sake, but for God's sake as well."[1]

Although we've focused on dealing with a particular sin in our lives that keeps tripping us up, we all know temptation also comes in every other area of life. Overcoming one besetting sin doesn't mean we're no longer under attack from our flesh and Satan.

Let's never forget that as long as we live in the body we'll face temptations to sin. Instead of sighing, "Well, what can I do, it's a losing battle," start praying for a hunger to be free from every kind of temptation—inner sins of pride and superiority, stubborn self-will, and jealousy, or outward acts of harmful gossip, sarcasm, and callous indifference to the feelings of others. God hasn't left us to resist on our own. He wants us to prepare ourselves for battle *before the temptation* so we can come through it without succumbing to sin. Let's look at ways to do this.

Be thankful. You are not left to fight the flesh on your own. Christ lives in you—He has forgiven you for every sin you've ever committed or *ever will*. Praise God for the new nature He has given you, one that desires to please Him above self. Thank Him each day that the Holy Spirit's presence in your life enables you to say *NO* to temptation.

Be alert. Avoid the bakery if gooey pastries are your downfall. Don't have long lunches or phone conversations with a gossip if you're trying to control what you say or think about others. If you are married but in the past have found yourself attracted to other men with a certain type of personality, when you meet one—run.

Analyze your weak areas and be alert for triggers that tempt you to sin. When you realize what they are, dump them— whether it's old photos or letters, possessions of various kinds, or lingering in certain places. Mean business with God, refusing to make excuses for what tempts you. To experience God's power over sin, we're responsible to "Count [ourselves] dead to sin but alive to God in Christ Jesus ... not [to] let sin reign in [our] mortal body ... not [to] offer the parts of [our] body to sin ... rather offer [ourselves] to God" (Romans 6:11-13).

Be self-controlled. We can be confident that self-control *is* possible because this is a fruit of the Holy Spirit. The closer we draw to the

Lord, growing in our love and desire to be obedient, the more this fruit becomes evident.

Although self-control comes from God, *we* need to exercise it. Remember, there are no magic wands in spiritual growth. God supplies the power, our part is to take hold of it. How can we do this? First, we turn to God, affirming, "Lord, I'm no longer a slave to sin, I'm alive to You. In Your power, I can and will do what pleases You." Then, we refuse to react to whatever tempts us, telling Satan, "By God's grace, you are not going to have the victory in my life."

Be realistic. Whatever tempts you to sin carries a sting in its tail. Pleasure quickly turns to pain and there's always a price to pay, even if our Enemy whispers otherwise.

The writer of Hebrews talks of Moses choosing to "share ill-treatment with God's people instead of enjoying the fleeting pleasures of sin" (11:25 TLB). Commenting on the phrase "the fleeting pleasures of sin," Chuck Swindoll writes, "What an eloquent expression—and true! Is sin pleasurable? You bet! It's so pleasurable that people will risk their reputations to taste its flavor. In doing so, all the efforts of our minds to alert us to sin's dangers are neutralized. We turn off the internal warnings as we turn on the desire."[2]

If lingering and longing cause us to switch off our minds to sin's dangers, we'd better flee as soon as we sense our attraction to the bait. Train yourself to resist before the bait is in front of you. Now is the time to think through the consequences, over and over. What might they be? Who will be hurt? What ideals will you betray? How will you feel about yourself and your relationship with God? What scorn will you bring to the name "Christian"? Be realistic about what you'll reap, before you find yourself caught up in the incredibly powerful—and subtle—pull of temptation.

Be equipped. Anyone who goes into battle without being equipped to fight is a fool headed to slaughter. So are we if we're not equipped for the spiritual battles facing us every day.

When Jesus faced the strongest temptations Satan could muster, He used the same weapon available to us. He repeatedly resisted Satan's enticements by saying, "It is written...." One of the most effective ways to either escape or bear up under temptation is to recall and act on the memorized Word. This source of spiritual power has been the secret of victory down through history. "I have hidden your word in my heart that I might not sin against you," wrote the Psalmist (119:11). Thinking Christians, serious about turning their stumbling blocks into stepping stones, do the same.

Equip yourself by memorizing verses that address your particular stumbling block. Is it pride, lust, greed, anger, or bitterness? Look up these words, or others similar to them, in a concordance. If you don't have one, ask at your church library, pastor's office, or Christian bookstore. Get equipped with the Word, then *use it as soon as you spy the bait.*

Take a moment to reflect on God's promise to provide either a way out of your temptation or the power to stand up under it. Do you believe this is true? Do you want His provision and power in your life? If you answer yes to both questions, what steps to freedom will you take *now*? Write down what God is directing you to do in order to turn your stumbling blocks into spiritual stepping stones.

Much as we wish tumbling from temptation into sin weren't a part of our lives, we know it is a constant possibility. When we do gulp the bait, guilt often causes us to ask, "Will God keep loving me even when I fail?"

Scripture responds with a thunderous YES! Among many affirmations of God's forgiveness, John ringingly declares, "If anybody does sin, we have one who speaks to the Father in our defense—Jesus Christ, the Righteous One. He is the atoning sacrifice for our sins" (1 John 2:1-2). What a relief! When we trip and fall, God says, "Get up." When we confess our sin, He forgives us. When we ask for spiritual renewal, He is already at work in our hearts.

I've Failed, Now What?

One of the most famous followers of God was King David. He is also one of the most famous sinners found in Scripture. After committing adultery with Bathsheba and fathering her child, David tried to cover his tracks. When that didn't work, he arranged for Bathsheba's husband, Uriah, to be killed. He then married Bathsheba, trying to act as if nothing happened—until God sent the prophet Nathan to confront him (2 Samuel 11-12:10).

David sinned big time, but he also repented sincerely and completely when faced with what he had done. Psalm 51 records both his sorrow for failing God as well as his strong trust that forgiveness and restoration were possible. God caused this Psalm to be included in Scripture for a reason—to encourage all of us who have stumbled but long to nestle close to Him once again. David's heart attitudes span the process of spiritual restoration. Let's learn from them in these verses:

1. *A needy heart* (Psalm 51:1-2). "Have mercy on me, O God.... Wash away all my iniquity and cleanse me from my sin." David was clearly heartbroken over his sin. He felt spiritually destitute and in great need of God's mercy and grace.

A needy heart is humble before God, makes no excuses, doesn't blame someone else or circumstances. Notice David didn't say, "Well, if she hadn't been on the rooftop this would never have happened." No, he acknowledged what he had chosen to do. Mourning over his sin, David looked to God for mercy and cleansing. Our journey back to joy begins with the same heart attitude.

2. *A submissive heart* (4). "Against you, you only, have I sinned and done what is evil in your sight." Ugly as it was, David confessed the truth. He had done evil in God's sight. He knew he deserved to be judged by Him.

David didn't make excuses for his behavior, nor did he find fault with God and accuse Him of being unjust. He submitted to God's standard of holiness, admitting honestly that he had failed miserably. When the Holy Spirit puts His finger on our hearts, let's not shrink from the truth He exposes to us. His purpose isn't to condemn and stir up guilt feelings, but to convict, cleanse, and restore us to spiritual vitality. This requires a submissive heart.

3. *An obedient heart* (10-12). Springing from a submissive heart is the longing to be obedient. Knowing he couldn't manufacture obedience on his own, David prayed, "Create in me a pure heart, O God, and renew a steadfast spirit within me ... grant me a willing spirit, to sustain me." David wanted to be radically committed to God, to have a single-minded desire to be obedient. He cried out to God not to take the Holy Spirit from him. He couldn't bear the thought of living in spiritual isolation, not knowing the joy of salvation or the constant presence of God in his life.

An obedient heart takes action on what the Holy Spirit reveals. When He shows us what needs to be dumped from our lives in order to quit stumbling again and again, out it goes. When He shows us what needs to be added, we act. The longing to please God changes talk into walk.

4. *An expectant heart* (13). After confessing his sins and seeking forgiveness, David didn't mope around believing his relationship with God was finished. He not only believed God would forgive him, he was confident God would restore him and use him for His purposes in the future. "Then I will teach transgressors your ways, and sinners will turn back to you."

One of Satan's tactics is to trick us into believing his lies. First, he tempts us to believe that biting the bait is no big deal. Then, when we do, he attacks with thoughts that God is through with us. Biting the bait *is* a big deal—Christ bore the penalty of that sin. But repentance frees us to be expectant. We can humbly, yet confidently, trust that cleansing and renewal will make us vessels God can and will use again.

5. *A resting heart* (16-17). David knew that what God wants most of all is our heart—not what we do, or achieve, or give to Him. "You do not delight in sacrifice, or I would bring it.... The sacrifices of God are a broken spirit, a broken and contrite heart, O God, you will not despise." We don't have to frantically find some way to prove to God how sorry we are, or swear on a stack of Bibles that we'll never fail again. God wants us to love Him, returning to Him with a broken and contrite heart when we fail. It's as simple as that.

Speaking of Jesus, the prophet Isaiah describes how He tenderly views all of us who aren't "super-saints." "A bruised reed he will not break, and a smoldering wick he will not snuff out" (42:3). He is our caring Shepherd, who seeks those who wander off. He is the Lord who loves us with an everlasting love. God *himself* has given us these truths, wrapped in picture language, to cherish and savor. He doesn't want us to remain locked in restless strivings or guilt-laden, imploring prayers for forgiveness. If we are His child, He invites us to rest—to joyfully embrace and delight in His love and acceptance. What could be more wonderful?

Can our stumbling blocks become stepping stones to a closer walk with God? With His help, they certainly can. Instead of sighing, *I wish I could be different*, take action. Open your eyes, look at your stumbling blocks:

Recognize what's behind them.

Remove what trips you up.

184

Run from the bait.

Ready yourself to resist before the assault comes—and

Rejoice at the opportunity every temptation offers to prove "greater is he who is in you, than he who is in the world."

Exciting changes are possible in spite of our trip-ups, blow-ups, and hang-ups.

Each of us is on a unique, God-shaped journey. God has been active in our lives, working out His plans and purposes—and He's still at work. But is it important to recall what He has done? To remember how He led, shaped, forgave, and loved us? Can looking back spur us on to spiritual maturity? Let's find out.

Reflections—for Thought and Discussion

1. What kind of temptation do you find yourself swimming around all too often?

2. How do you feel when you tumble into temptation? What do you tell yourself?

3. What insights did you discover by answering the quiz questions? How can you benefit in a practical way from this knowledge?

4. What do you learn about temptation from the following verses: Genesis 2:15-3:13; Matthew 4:1-11; Luke 22:46: James 1:13-15?

5. Try to think of as many resources as possible that God provides to help you resist sin. Which have you found to be particularly helpful?

6. Has wrestling with a temptation helped you to grow spiritually stronger? How?

Memory Verse

"We do not have a high priest who is unable to sympathize with our weaknesses, but we have one who has been tempted in every way, just as we are—yet was without sin" (Hebrews 4:15).

Notes:

1 Erwin Lutzer, *How to Say No to a Stubborn Habit* (Wheaton, Ill.: Victor Books, 1979), 50.

2 Charles R. Swindoll, *Three Steps Forward, Two Steps Back* (Nashville: Thomas Nelson Publishers, 1980), 99.

TEN

How Will Looking Back Spur Me Forward?

WHEN AN ENGLISH CHURCH VICAR DISCOVERED HIS
CAT STUCK high in a tree, he was forced to mount a perilous
rescue operation. Climbing as far as his ladder would take him, he
discovered he still couldn't reach the family pet.

Not to be defeated, he tied one end of a rope to the trunk of the tree
at the highest point he could reach and the other to the tree toward
the ground so the cat could jump to safety—the inevitable
happened. The rope broke and the cat was catapulted into space.

No more was heard of the poor creature until a couple of weeks
later. The minister was in the supermarket when he saw one of his
church members buying cat food. Overcome with nostalgia, he
remarked that he hadn't realized her family had a cat.

"We didn't until two weeks ago," she replied. "It's all a bit of a
miracle, really. I was having a picnic on the lawn with my daughter
when she said, 'Mummy, I'd like to have a cat.'

"'You'll have to ask Jesus for one,' I told her. And at that very
moment this cat came flying through the air and landed on the
lawn next to us. He's been staying with us ever since."

No doubt whenever mother or daughter looked at their divinely
delivered cat, they marveled at God's unique demonstration of His
power. Their new pet was a living memorial to God's reality.

How about you? Can you look back at some event in your life and
say, "God definitely proved His reality to me that time"?

Most of us don't have living memorials to God's reality purring
around our homes. We have to rely on memory. The older we get,

the trickier this becomes because we have so much more stuff crammed in our heads. More difficult still is retrieving what we're sure is in there. One young man from England, by the way, will never have this problem. Gifted with remarkable recall from childhood, he set a world record by reciting all four of the Gospels from memory. This feat took him ten hours—allowing himself ten minute breaks between Gospels and thirty minutes for lunch.

For the rest of us more normal folk, the ability to remember varies. My memory both depresses and amazes me. Staring at a good friend while desperately trying to remember her name is as startling an experience as meeting an old acquaintance and remembering details told to me twenty years before. Each day has its surprises.

Forgetting people's names, my phone number, and where I parked my car at the mall are nuisances. But we can easily forget something of far greater consequence—how God personally and powerfully cares for us. Have your experiences of God stayed in your mind over the years? Do you remember your first days as a Christian? Your first taste of seeing God work out a situation for you? The excitement you felt at seeing "coincidences" where a person, event, or book met a precise need and you realized God was real and cared about you?

God *is* concerned with who we are. He *is* involved with our lives. After our new birth, He began to shape our character and direction in life through growth experiences, crises, and challenges. These personal experiences of God, like a well from which we can constantly drink, spiritually refresh us—but only if we remember to look back and draw from them.

Take Time to Remember

Thinking about what God has done isn't a trip down memory lane where we sit with a box of Kleenex and get ready to sniffle as nostalgia overcomes us. Yes, some tears might come, and for me they quite often do. But God wants us to remember for more important reasons—so that we might grow in faith, trust, and commitment to Him every time we are reminded of His greatness.

When His people Israel crossed into the Promised Land He taught them an unforgettable first lesson. After the Israelites crossed the River Jordan under Joshua's leadership, God told them to stop and build a memorial before moving on to conquer the land. There was no better way to fix in their minds the miracle God had just performed on their behalf: even though the Jordan raged at flood stage, the water stopped flowing, piling up in a heap a great distance away. The priests carrying the ark stood on dry ground in the middle of the riverbed while all Israel crossed safely. When every person had passed over, one man from each of the twelve tribes took up a stone—probably a large one he would need to heave up on his shoulder—from the middle of the river. A short time later, under the Lord's direction, Joshua piled up these stones to serve as a memorial to God's power (Joshua 3:15-17; 4).

How easy it would have been to just keep marching—to say a brief "thanks" and file the memory in the back of their minds until it no longer filled them with awe. But God said, "No!" They weren't to simply press on with their lives without paying attention to what He had done. He told them to build a memorial, "so that all the peoples of the earth might know that the hand of the Lord is powerful and so that you might always fear the Lord your God."

Caught up in our own hectic schedules—drop one child off at gymnastics, another at swimming lessons, finish that overdue project, plan dinner, stop at the cleaners, run into the grocery store—we're just as prone as the Israelites to move on quickly without reflecting on what God has done for us. But just as it mattered to God that the Israelites remembered what He had done for them, so it matters to Him that we remember His involvement in our lives.

Remember What Builds You Up

The Bible contains numerous commands to *remember* or *forget not*. "Remember the former things, those of long ago; I am God, and there is no other" (Isaiah 46:9); "Remember the wonders he has done, his miracles" (Psalm 105.5); "Remember the words I spoke to you" (John 15:20); "Praise the Lord, O my soul, and forget not all his benefits" (Psalm 103:2). Notice that everything we're told to remember reflects God's goodness and glory and builds us up. Learning from past experiences falls within this category.

When Marilyn and her husband, Ian, went on a two-week holiday with another couple, Jan and Todd, she never suspected what could happen. In contrast to Ian, who seldom noticed such things, Todd warmly complimented her taste in clothes and interest in the local culture. Soon they were laughing together, sitting beside each other, feeling the strong pull of unexpected sexual attraction.

"I was shocked at how attracted I could become to a man who complimented me and made me laugh," she confided later. "How could I, a committed Christian, become so vulnerable? Thank God nothing happened. I did learn an important lesson, though," she said. "I discovered where I'm weak. Having learned from my one close call, I now avoid as much as possible lingering in the company of any man who attracts me."

Past experiences can be powerful teachers if we learn from them. But we need to watch out that we don't dwell on our weaknesses, opening the door to either fresh battles with temptation or attacks of guilt. Nor are we to look back, allowing memories of any ugliness, abuse, or injustice we've suffered to drag us into depression or renewed bitterness.

The apostle Paul stated emphatically that he would not live in the past. Did that mean he never looked back and rejoiced over God's calling and leading? Of course not. Paul talked constantly of what

God had done in his life, His mercy in saving him, standing by him, and commissioning him to spread the gospel. What he chose to forget was all that once filled him with pride and arrogance—his background, upbringing, and self-righteousness. In fact, he counted them as rubbish compared with the wonder of knowing the risen Lord. Even his guilt over hounding the early Christians to prison and death was left in the past. These were aspects of who he once was. They no longer defined the person he now was in Christ (Philippians 3:7-14).

God tells us to "Forget the former things; do not dwell on the past. See, I am doing a new thing!" (Isaiah 43:18-19). In looking back, distinguish between what God wants you to forget and what He wants you to remember. He doesn't want you to be dragged down into the muck and mire of the past, to reopen old wounds—He calls you to see the new things He is doing in your life. So look back without dread—remember what He has done for you—and let your spirit soar in joy and gratitude, aware that you are forgiven and deeply loved.

Remember and Grow

Remembering plays a powerful role in our lives. Looking back at our spiritual history—how God came to our rescue, comforted us, answered prayer, gave us strength to persevere— opens our eyes to what we might not have seen at the time. We begin to:

* *Recognize God's providence*—places where He divinely overruled in certain situations, or put people in our lives to meet a need or provide guidance.

* *Recognize God's training*—events and experiences that once puzzled us become more understandable as we see how our character was shaped by them.

* *Recognize God's purposes*—opportunities God opened to us, how He gifted us with particular abilities or impressed us to go in a certain direction.

What's the result of looking back at God's hand on our lives? Praise wells up, our perspective changes, and our passion to walk with Him is renewed. Remembering spurs our faith into action and strengthens our confidence that God indeed is active in our lives.

You may have followed Jesus for a few months or many decades. And perhaps your memories are more of your failures and God's loving forgiveness than of great victories. But regardless of how long you've followed Him or how little or much growth you have experienced, tracing God's love is a surefire way to put the sparkle back into your spiritual life.

How does this happen? As the Holy Spirit guides our thinking to the many ways we've experienced God's goodness, He also stirs our hearts. Fanning the flame of our love for God, He fills us with overflowing thankfulness and a longing to be more devoted to the Lord than we were before. The end result is spiritual renewal—worship, praise, a hunger to walk in obedience, and the desire to sing and rejoice over the greatness and goodness of God.

Tracing God's Fingerprints

Do you want to experience some spiritual fire? To taste a fresh passion and delight in God? Then begin to trace God's fingerprints on your life, starting with a look at your roots.

Significant Beginnings

Spiritual roots. If you ask your Christian friends why they came to faith in Christ, you're likely to get a potpourri of answers:

* My mother taught me about sin and Jesus' dying for me when I was a small child and I simply believed.

* I had a guilty conscience, so when a friend told me how to have peace with God, I received Christ.

* I was confused and lonely. When I heard the incredible news that God loved me and gave His Son for me, I responded right away.

* I never bought the idea that this world just happened—that we're here through some cosmic accident. I was open to the idea that there is a God because we're just too complex for there to be no designer. When a friend I admire shared her faith, I began investigating Christianity and became a believer in Jesus.

Talking with friends about how we came into God's family is awe-inspiring. Just imagine. The eternal God of the Universe—all-powerful, all-knowing, all-loving—knew about us, specks of dust on an out-of-the-way planet. And more than that, He cared enough to reach out to each of us with our varied needs, hang-ups, and questions. What could be a more significant beginning to remember and rejoice over? Does your first date come close? Your first job? Your wedding day?

Has it been a while since you've marveled over God's intervention in your life? Stop and thank Him. Recall the cost of your salvation. Reflect on how your purpose and direction in life has changed because of His love. Let your heart be stirred as you think of your destiny—to be with Christ and to be like Him forever. Look back and say, "I will remember the deeds of the Lord; yes, I will remember your miracles of long ago. I will meditate on all your works and consider all your mighty deeds" (Psalm 77:11-12).

Family roots. What are your most vivid childhood memories? Are they like Judy's? She grew up in a Christian family with a stay-at-home, fun-loving mom, a dad who came home for dinner every night, and brothers who watched over her. Now in her fifties, Judy cheerfully acknowledges she's just like her mother. Because her joyful attitude is so appealing, she's a prized friend and employee.

Maybe your early environment was at the other end of the spectrum. Perhaps you identify more with Jennifer who, decades later, is still working through the effects of growing up in an alcoholic home. You might even share similar experiences to Angela whose parents beat her regularly, yet could still walk into church smiling every Sunday. For many of us, family memories contain both negative and positive experiences—as do mine.

My most vivid memories are of my mother's fiery disposition. She ignited some explosive moments in our family, but her passionate nature also flew to the rescue of hurting or needy people.

Because my father served in the Royal Air Force most of his working life, I spent many years as a child living in Third World countries. Growing up surrounded by heart-wrenching poverty, I watched my mother frequently slip small packages of food and clothing to people who had little or nothing. Whenever we walked past a beggar, Mum would whisper to my father, "Give the poor man something." After she died, my two sisters and I went through her clothes closet and were amazed to find so few items. When we asked Dad where all her clothes were, he answered, "Oh, you know your mother. She was always coming across someone who didn't have much so she'd give them one of her blouses or a dress."

Did God use these powerful early experiences to benefit me? Are they something I can thank Him for? Yes. Even though I copied my mother's example of blowing up when I felt frustrated and overwhelmed, God used it for good. By constantly failing in this area and crying out for the power to be different, my need drove me to depend on God—something that might not have happened without such a desperate struggle. On the positive side, I am grateful for the influence my mother's tender heart and compassion for others has had on me.

When we look back at both the negative and positive influences on our lives, it's clear that God wastes nothing that happens to us. Our significant early experiences may not be what we would choose, but God's purposes are the same—to take hold of whatever has influenced us and use it as a tool to shape our spiritual development.

As you look back at your family life, think about how you were influenced and shaped by what you experienced. Write down what comes to mind, both negative and positive.

How has God used these early influences to help you mature in Christ?

What does this show you about His power and intent to bring good out of both the negative and positive aspects of your past?

Significant People

Have you ever looked back and realized that God knew who you needed in your life before you had a clue? Or that He uses people to show us He knows and cares about where we are and what we're facing. As you look back, you may begin to marvel at God's providence in your life—His ability not only to see but also to meet your need through certain people who influenced you at precisely the right time.

Help and Hope Givers

Paula knew her marriage was in trouble. In fact, she was so depressed over the constant bickering between Jack and her that she doubted they could survive much longer as husband and wife. In the midst of her worry, she met an older couple at a neighborhood party and learned that the husband was a former pastor.

"A few days later I felt I just had to talk to someone or I was going to crack up," confided Paula. "Suddenly, thoughts of this older couple came to my mind. I sensed that maybe they could help me.

I didn't know who else to turn to, so I asked my neighbor for their phone number. I called and asked if they could come over that night because my husband was out of town. When they arrived an hour later, they were both carrying their Bibles. I can't explain why, but I suddenly felt a surge of hope.

"During the next hour they listened patiently as I poured out all our conflicts and my sense of hopelessness. There weren't any solutions that I could see. Even though I don't remember much else of what they said, I've never forgotten one question I think the husband asked, 'Don't you think God can change your situation?'

"Crazy as it sounds now, this possibility had not occurred to me. I never saw that couple again, but their words gave me what I desperately needed—hope to keep holding on. And do you know what?" asked Paula, her face breaking into a delighted smile. "In God's time, our relationship did change through much prayer, honest discussion of our needs and expectations, and a willingness to consider each other's feelings and viewpoint."

God uses many different people to shape our lives and guide us into His paths. Think about who woke you up to Christ. Did someone suggest going to a particular church where you spiritually flourished? Did someone take you along to a Bible study that opened your eyes to God's truth? Or did someone lovingly stick with you and not let you give up when you felt completely hopeless about life?

Let your mind linger on the ways God has revealed His presence to you. Can you recall His bringing a significant person along at just the time you needed help or hope? How does this strengthen your faith in God's ability to help you today?

Divine Contacts

Another way God uses people to show us His personal involvement is through "divine contacts," people He sends across our path at crucial moments in our spiritual development. A "divine contact" might be a more mature believer who sees our desire for God and challenges us to a greater intimacy with Him. Or they might affirm a gift they see in us, urging us to develop it. They might also be God's instrument to change our direction by opening doors God plans for us to enter. This was Philip's experience.

Sent by the Spirit to the desert road between Jerusalem and Gaza, Philip noticed an Ethiopian sitting in his chariot reading the book of Isaiah. The Spirit told Philip to go closer. Upon inquiring whether the man understood what he was reading, Philip was invited up into the chariot to explain God's message. The result was the Ethiopian's conversion and the spread of the gospel to his country. Philip had been a "divine contact" God placed in the path of someone He wanted to reach (Acts 8:26-40).

Joyce was a "divine contact" God used in my life. We hardly knew each other when she asked me to consider teaching the women's Bible study at her church for a year. This contact led her to give my name to a local Bible college to teach in their evening school.

From the material developed for the two classes I taught, I was invited to join a team putting together a book on women's ministries. This in turn led to an invitation to speak at *Winning Women,* a statewide conference in Michigan. After my second visit to this conference, the organizers sent tapes of my talks to Australia. A year later an invitation came from a women's interdenominational organization asking me to speak all over that continent for six weeks. From that event came invitations to speak in England, Malaysia, and New Zealand. God's thoughts and ways are always beyond ours!

God used Joyce to open the door to a whole new direction, His direction, for my life. The "divine contacts" God has brought into your life might have kicked off a short or a long chain of events, but they fulfill God's purpose for you at that time. Perhaps you've also experienced the excitement of being used by God in someone else's life.

As you look back on your Christian journey, can you see where God brought a "divine contact" across your path—a person whose words, affirmation, or challenge affected your life? What happened?

Has God used you as a "divine contact" in someone's life? Take a moment to write a short prayer thanking Him for this privilege.

Spiritual Role Models

"Remember your leaders, who spoke the word of God to you. Consider the outcome of their way of life and imitate their faith" (Hebrews 13:7). Spiritual role models aren't always recognized leaders or teachers in the formal sense of the word. However, they most definitely speak the word of God to us—by example.

Some of the most significant people in our lives are those God has used to spur us on in our desire for Him. Their influence might have come by modeling a simple yet profound love for Jesus Christ, through acts of kindness, or by way of words of teaching or encouragement. Probably none considered themselves "spiritual role models." They were simply living out their faith.

Claribel, Flo, and Beth bustled around the church kitchen getting food heated up for a Sunday potluck. Holding my son, Elliot, in my arms, I watched as they chatted and laughed with all the other helpers. When the meal was over, no clean-up crew appeared. These same women cheerfully did the dishes. And they served in this way every time the church hosted a meal. What influence did their unselfish service have on me? I found myself glad to pitch in and serve the Lord with the same spirit of joy.

A few weeks after moving to a new church, I silently prayed one Sunday morning that someone would reach out and help us to overcome our feeling of being outsiders. Minutes later Ellie approached, asking if we were free to go home with her family for lunch. Her cheerful hospitality showed me how God can use our homes as a powerful tool to encourage others. Her example fired my desire to open our home to others.

Dave's love for the Lord and knowledge of Scripture was apparent. So was his willingness to answer a young woman's questions and encourage her spiritual growth. Passing on Christian books and magazines with a casual "I think you'll find this helpful," he fulfilled his role as a godly elder and a spiritual role model. He noticed and affirmed one unimportant sheep. Not only am I grateful, I want to follow in his footsteps.

People very different from each other contribute to our growth. Some are famous missionaries, speakers, Bible teachers, and writers. Many others are fairly ordinary, everyday people like us. As you think back over the significant people God has brought into your life, who comes to mind? What did they do that made a lasting impact on your life?

Significant Experiences

Quick! What significant experiences flash into your mind? High school or college graduation? Getting married? A trip to Europe? A severe illness or loss of someone you loved? If we're alive and alert, life has many of these moments forever etched into our memories. And if we're alive and alert Christians, our spiritual lives will also contain not-to-be-forgotten experiences.

Think of some mountaintop encounter you've had with God. Or lessons that came from tripping up spiritually and going "splat" in the mud of life. Do you recall battling with God over some issue? Or taking a scary step of blind obedience and marveling afterward at how He took you through? What about a time of stress, crisis, and loss where God's presence held you together? Every significant experience we go through holds the seed of growth within it. Whether delightful or difficult, God's purpose is to utilize them to accomplish His purposes— to teach us, change our character, and deepen our relationship with Him.

The longer we walk with God, the more He gives us memorable experiences. These "God and me" memories become part of our spiritual heritage. We need to progress beyond remembering, however—the *past* is fertile ground from which to learn essential lessons for *today* and *tomorrow*. Linda discovered this as she looked back at a painful time in her life.

Learning About God

"I never realized back then that Andy, my boyfriend in college, meant more to me than God," said Linda. "I adored him and would have done anything to marry him, but he wasn't ready to tie himself to one person. I remember pleading with God to make it work, but in the end Andy walked away.

"One day, years later, I remembered how heartbroken I had been. I prayed, 'God, let me understand why You didn't give me what I so desperately wanted.'" Linda hesitated before asking, "Do you know what He brought to my mind? That Andy had been an idol in my life. I had let him take God's place.

"I realize now that no matter how much I begged, God wasn't about to give me what I idolized. He wanted first place in my heart and wasn't going to share His rightful position with anyone else. As I matured in my faith, putting Him first became my greatest longing."

What was the result of Linda's more mature hindsight? She could now see what had remained hidden from her for many years—God had said no to her pleading prayers because He knew it was not for her best. Besides coming to peace with her past, Linda's trust in God's sovereign control was strengthened and she learned to think carefully—before she asked.

As you recall past experiences, what truths about *God* have you learned from them? How do these help you today?

Learning About Yourself

Evelyn went through a different kind of indelible experience. She found herself embroiled in a painful conflict.

"I went back and forth for many weeks between a strong desire to hit back and wanting to let the Lord take care of my reputation," she confided. "The fact that it was other Christians who attacked me made the situation even more painful. But as I kept praying, the Lord showed me that refusing to let bitterness rule my life was far more important than showing them how wrong they were.

"As I look back, I realize how patiently God taught me. I've learned that conflicts and crises don't have to be pointless, miserable failures. They can be extremely profitable if we learn from them. Not only did I gain some valuable insights into myself, I also learned some lessons about building relationships.

Most of all, this experience drew me closer to the Lord and caused my dependence on Him to grow."

Can you identify with Evelyn? Take a moment to reflect on a difficult experience in your past. What did you learn from it? How has this helped you grow in your *understanding of God* and *yourself*?

Significant Blessings

When did you last look back and jump for joy at how God has blessed you? Well, maybe you didn't whoop it up, shout, "Yes!" and pump your arm up and down—but hopefully you felt happy and managed to whisper, "Thank you, Lord." Remembering lessons learned through difficult experiences is important, but that isn't the whole picture by any means. You shall "remember how the Lord your God led you all the way ..." (Deuteronomy 8:2). "All the way" includes exciting experiences of blessing, answered prayer, unexpected joys, and the many good gifts we've all received—all worth getting a little worked up over.

"Count your blessings, name them one by one, and it will surprise you what the Lord has done," says the old hymn. It's true. God showers His love upon us and He wants us to notice and be thankful. "Give thanks to Him and praise His Name," we're instructed.

Why? Because "the Lord is good and His love endures forever" (Psalm 100:5). When we do this, He is glorified, our spiritual "blahs" get blown to pieces, and faith and delight in Him blossoms.

Remembering His blessings kicks off a whole chain of spiritually powerful effects: thanksgiving, a joyful spirit, confidence in God, and renewed commitment to trust His leading. Count your blessings—don't just remember events, but trace God's finger along the map of your journey. Spontaneously worship Him as you spot the many evidences of His love and care. To do this, think back. Has He caused someone to:

* provide money or some other need when you were sick, out of work, or struggling?

* invite you home for a meal, give you somewhere to stay, be a listening ear?

* encourage you through a word, note, or phone call at the exact time of your need?

* offer you a job, invite you into a ministry, recommend you for a promotion?

* love you in spite of your flaws and failings?

* model a Christlike life before you, stimulating your desire for God?

* be your friend, standing up for you even in your worst moments?

These are all ways God shows us His reality. He uses people to shout, "I know where you are and what you're dealing with!" But He also blesses us in ways that leave no doubt that *He*—not just the people He uses to touch us directly—brought this about.

Faced with a need to get back to the States quickly for a specialist's appointment, I prayed fervently for a seat on Friday's full flight out of Singapore. "We have a seat available," the airline clerk affirmed two days before flight time. Delighted by this answer to prayer, I called Jim and told him what God had done. Two hours later the same airline clerk called back to say, "I'm very sorry, but your type of ticket doesn't allow you to leave on a Friday. I have a seat available the following Tuesday. Do you want it?"

Did I want it? No! I wanted a seat on Friday's plane—but nothing would make the airline personnel bend the rules.

Arriving at Los Angeles airport on my way to Portland the next Tuesday, I maneuvered my way through the crowds sitting, standing, and even lying on the floor. "I'm booked on the eleven a.m. flight to Portland," I told the reservation clerk at my gate.

"Well, you're very lucky, ma'am," he responded. "The Portland airport has been closed since Friday due to a severe ice storm and your flight is the first one going in since then."

I stood there for a few seconds, stunned. God had kept me from coming on the Friday flight. He had supernaturally intervened and protected me from being stranded in Los Angeles. All the events of the previous weeks that had left me exhausted both physically and emotionally were known to Him—my father's unexpected hospitalization in England, his death while I was in flight from Singapore to London, the pain of not being there to see him one last time, guilt feelings at delaying my departure due to an important commitment because I was so sure he would pull through.

God knew I didn't need to learn a painful lesson, that time. Instead, I needed to sense the comfort of His loving arms wrapped around me and holding me up. Sitting on the flight to Portland, I worshiped silently, deeply touched by God's tender, personal awareness of my fragile state.

Blessings surround us every day. Good health, available healthcare, shelter, food, and other necessities of life are all gifts from Him. So are people—family, friends, our local church fellowship, co-workers. Look around at all God has blessed you with and give Him thanks. Look back, savor the memories of His touch on your life, and worship. Write down your spiritually sweet memories in the back of your Bible or in a journal. Treasure them and let the past spur you forward into greater awareness of God's reality and care.

Are you excited now that you can recognize God's hand on your life? Well, you can experience still more of His reality in the days ahead.

In spite of our feelings of inadequacy, obvious flaws, and times of failure, God gives us work to do. In fact, He created us to do good works. We might not be spiritual "super-saints" but that's no excuse—God wants us to serve Him. Let's discover why and how, as well as what happens when we say yes.

Reflections—for Thought and Discussion

1. How has God made himself real to you. What encouragement do you find in these memories?

2. As you look back, where have you seen God's providence at work bringing people, events, or resources into your path at the right time? How do you see this activity of God in the following: Genesis 2:18; Exodus 4:13-16; Ruth 1:15-19; 1 Kings 19:1-9? What does this tell you about God?

3. In what ways has God used your spiritual or family roots to draw you closer to himself?

4. What helpful thoughts or lessons did you find in the section *Significant People*?

5. Who has God provided to give you hope or help in the past? Who is His gift to you right now? This week, look for a way to let them know what they mean to you.

6. How does looking back at God's faithfulness encourage you in a situation you face today? As you think about the future, how are you helped by remembering all the ways He has led you so far?

Memory Verse

"I will remember the deeds of the Lord; yes, I will remember your miracles of long ago. I will meditate on all your works and consider all your mighty deeds" (Psalm 77:11-12).

ELEVEN

You Really Want *Me* to Serve *You*?

THERE ARE MANY REASONS WHY GOD SHOULDN'T HAVE called you. But don't worry. You're in good company:

Moses stuttered ... David's armor didn't fit.

Timothy had ulcers ... Hosea's wife was a prostitute.

Amos's only training was in the school of fig-tree pruning ... Jacob was a liar.

David had an affair ... Solomon was too rich.

Abraham was too old ... David was too young.

Peter was afraid of death ... Lazarus was dead.

John was self-righteous ... Naomi was a widow.

Paul was a murderer ... so was Moses.

Jonah ran away from God ... Miriam was a gossip.

Gideon and Thomas both doubted ... Jeremiah was depressed and suicidal.

Elijah was burned out ... Martha was a worrywart.

Samson had long hair ... Noah got drunk.

Did I mention that Moses had a short fuse?

So did Peter, Paul—well, God called lots of folks who did.

—Anonymous

Whew! After that lot, what excuse do we have for mumbling, "Oh, God couldn't use me!" Yes, He can—and He wants to. Do you know what would have happened to the growth of the church if God had limited himself to using those people *we* consider suitable? Not much!

Think of all the Christian ministries that wouldn't exist if God used only deeply spiritual "super-saints," highly talented people with Master's degrees in Servantology, or those who win awards for being Ms. or Mr. Dynamically Successful at Everything. Who would teach the basics to baby Christians, encourage the lonely, help young moms cope, take meals to the sick, befriend hurting teens, assist ex-prisoners to get back on their feet, or—the list of needy people is endless.

Consider your own experience. How many of the people who taught, influenced, and encouraged you were perfect, all-together, halo-topped "super-saints"? Probably none—because they don't exist. So where do these facts leave us? Facing the scary yet exciting possibilities of God working through us, the imperfect and struggling, to touch other people's lives for His good purposes.

We might have to scratch our heads to think of what abilities we have to offer. But regardless of how *we* estimate our usefulness to God, He knows what we can do *if He empowers us.*

Qualifications Needed: An Available Heart

Have you ever gone for a job interview and wondered if you had the right qualifications for the position? Or squirmed inside as the interviewer fixed his steely gaze on you and said, "Now just what do you have to offer our company?" Or maybe there's an acute need in some area of your church for helpers, but even though you'd like to help, you're convinced they wouldn't want you. After all, what can you do?

Probably most of us, the non-"super-saints," have been there. One summer an appeal went out for cooks to work in our church's camp kitchen. Now, this is not where I shine. My friends who can mix huge batches of dough and have them miraculously rise up into loaves of bread have my deep admiration. I'm better known for producing leaden weights than loaves of whole wheat bread. Even my husband once accidentally blurted out, "Are these stones?" as I served him a plate of scones. (He claims I misheard him.)

Nevertheless, cooks were needed at camp. I was available that week and felt inclined to help, so I rather nervously volunteered. After hearing about my abilities, they kindly assigned me to the perfect job—peeling potatoes and chopping onions. I had a great time.

A well-known phrase says, "God is less interested in our ability than in our availability." This isn't an out-of-date cliché but a powerful truth. Look again at the motley collection of characters God enlisted into His service—none of them without shortcomings. Some even came up with all sorts of excuses, strenuously resisting God's call. Yet He used each of them with their unique mix of backgrounds and talents to accomplish exactly what He had in mind.

Now, look around at your own church or Christian outreach in your community. Who's serving there? Schoolteachers, computer techs, truck drivers, nurses, business people, grandmothers, homemakers? A mix of people only God could pull together. What do they have in common? A love for Jesus Christ, an available heart, and trust that *God can make them able* for whatever He calls them to do.

Gladys Aylward is one woman who vividly proved that an available heart is more important to God than money, education, or intellectual ability. Gladys lived in the earlier part of this century and longed to serve God on the mission field. But she was a poor, uneducated English woman with little to offer.

Gladys's lack of education created what seemed an impossible barrier. Despite her desperate efforts to learn, she found the classes at the China Inland Mission Training School beyond her abilities. None of her teachers felt she could ever master the complex Chinese language. After three months, the school's superintendent gently suggested that she return to her former employment as a parlor maid.

Far from being discouraged, Gladys's belief that God had called her to China intensified. But how could it ever happen? Rejected by the mission's training school, she determined that with God's help and her own hard work she would get herself to China. Gladys bought herself a one-way, third-class ticket on the Trans-Siberian Railway to Vladivostok in October 1932. She then took one ship to Japan and another to China. Her final mode of transportation into the interior was by mule.

Learning Chinese by mimicking what she heard, Gladys used her flair for dramatic storytelling to share the gospel. When wars raged across China, God had another extraordinary task for His brave servant. Displaying her great faith in God and her tremendous courage, she led hundreds of orphaned children through the war-torn country to a place of safety. Her life story is told in the book *The Small Woman* as well as in the movie *Inn of the Sixth Happiness.*[1]

Saved to Serve

None of us are saved to sit and soak in spiritual blessings, to stuff ourselves with scriptural teachings, or to sigh over the decline of our churches or country and do nothing about it. We're saved to enjoy a love relationship with the living God. But this is never an end in itself. Out of love for God surges a great desire to serve Him in His power and for His glory. We might never be called to some faraway place as Gladys Aylward was, but if we want to change, to become what we're not, to grow spiritually strong, our love for God must move us to act as He leads.

One mark of a growing Christian is service—doing something for someone else, saying yes to God's nudges to get involved in His priorities, sacrificing your time, resources, even your reputation, in order to help others. Instead of majoring on our own self-fulfillment, Jesus, the greatest servant of all, calls us to follow His example. As God, He didn't sit up in heaven keeping His distance from the difficulties and pain we experience. He laid aside His privileges, hid His splendor and glory, and came to our rescue. Seeing our need and inability to help ourselves, He came to serve us—even though it meant going all the way to the Cross (Philippians 2:5-11).

How are we to follow in His steps? Merely noticing needs isn't enough. Nor is praying that God will fill vacancies in the Sunday school teaching staff, provide more greeters at the church door, or prompt others to paint rooms at the local rescue mission.

Being realistic, these particular jobs may not suit us. We'd make a disastrous Sunday school teacher, never get to the church on time to greet anyone, or can't paint without making a huge mess. But there are numerous other ways we can follow in His steps. We can get involved in serving others according to our own giftings. I saw a touching illustration of this when I volunteered at a crisis pregnancy center.

A white-haired, plainly dressed woman walked quietly up to the front desk. She pulled several pairs of knitted booties out of her bag. "I wondered if you could pass these on to some of the young mothers you help," she said softly. "I walk past your center quite often and wanted to help in some way. I hope you can use these."

She slipped away as quietly as she'd come in. I stood there dabbing my tears as I thought of this sweet lady. Because of her love for God, she was still bearing fruit in her old age.

When we see opportunities to serve in some way, let's remember that God *has* given us gifts to use for Him. We have no grounds for making excuses, volunteering someone else, or whispering shyly, "Oh, I couldn't possibly do that. I really have nothing to offer." Yes, we do.

Serving God might cost us very little, but be prepared. Sometimes it can mean allowing our lives to be invaded and disrupted by the needs of others. This was Jenny's experience when a friend asked for her help.

"When Carol appeared at our front door, I could sense something was wrong," Jenny related. "I invited her in and then listened as she told me her counselor had advised her to separate from her husband because of his abusive actions." Jenny and Jack opened their hearts and their home to this woman.

Carol and her young daughter stayed with Jenny and Jack for several weeks before deciding what to do next. While trying to help her friend make it through each day, Jenny was stung by other people's criticism for taking Carol in.

"Some people felt that by allowing Carol to stay with us, we were encouraging the breakup of her marriage," said Jenny sadly. "This wasn't at all true, of course. We prayed it would somehow come together again, but in the end they did divorce."

Taking Carol into their home disrupted Jenny and Jack's lives in many ways. Would they do it again? "Absolutely," responded Jenny. "Jack and I felt responsible before the Lord to help someone in such distress. There will always be those who criticize, but in the end we have to stand before the Lord. We will answer to Him, not them. I'm glad we agreed to be available."

How about you? Are you available to serve God in various ways? What would you answer if Jesus asked you?

But Who Am I Supposed to Serve?

Thousands of years before studies proved that those who actively help others have a more positive outlook on life, God instructed His people, "Love your neighbor as yourself." Have you ever wondered who exactly fits this description?

Surely God doesn't mean that scary-looking kid who lives two doors away with rings sprouting through his nose, a pierced eyebrow, and punk hairdo—does He? Aren't our neighbors people like us—you know, more normal types?

That Person Is My Neighbor?

In telling the story of the Good Samaritan, Jesus made it clear that our neighbor is anyone who is in need. Whether he or she looks alarming, practices an alternative lifestyle, drips with diamonds, or cherishes New Age crystals, God calls us to love and serve them by meeting their needs. In *Becoming a Contagious Christian*, Bill Hybels writes, "One of the primary reasons God calls His followers to be extraordinarily caring people is because acts of mercy open up people's hearts like nothing else can."[2]

Authentic Christians are God's agents for change, both physical and spiritual. Just think about what is actually happening when you and I, energized by our love for God, step out of our comfort zone to help others. Living through us, Jesus pours out His love, rescues, heals, and transforms those for whom He died. And we are allowed to be part of what He is doing. What an honor.

Family Ties

Anyone in need makes them our neighbor. Christians, however, have an even more intimate responsibility to care for each other. We're God's family. We're part of one body. Whatever our gender, ethnic group, or economic status, we belong to one another. We're all equally precious in God's sight. More than that, like any family, we're to rejoice, comfort, encourage, and serve one another.

God never intended the church to be like going to the movies—where we ignore everyone around us, watch the show, and go home. *We* are the church. We're to get involved in each other's lives—not only on Sundays but throughout the week—be there when someone needs help, and support what God is doing through our congregation, the fellowship of believers.

What does "Love your neighbor as yourself" and "being part of the family of God" mean in practical terms? First, to know that God's plan is to enlist you and me to serve Him both inside and outside the Christian community. Second, to realize He is able to make us capable of doing His will beyond anything we think possible. And third, to believe He has in mind tailor-made situations we've never dreamed of where we'll accomplish the good works He's planned for us all along.

Breathtaking, isn't it! Do you sense the exciting possibilities for growth and development when you sign up to serve Him? Unthought of opportunities lie before each of us. And as long as we keep saying yes to God, they'll spice up our lives, fill us with unequaled satisfaction, and stretch our faith while we experience how God can use us.

Scripture is full of information about this important part of living for God. We don't have to stumble around in the dark wondering if we've been called, if we're equipped, and where on earth we're supposed to serve. The Bible is clear: Every Christian is called, equipped by the Holy Spirit, and has good works to accomplish for God. Now that we've established these basic truths, let's look in more detail at what they mean.

I'm Called. But Where Is the Burning Bush?

Have you ever stopped to watch a burning bush and heard a voice speaking to you? What about walking along a road and being blinded by a light as bright as the noonday sun? Has the angel Gabriel ever appeared to you and given *you* a personal message from God?

If we haven't had these startling experiences, how are we supposed to know if we've been called to serve God? Surely it wouldn't be difficult for God to arrange for us mere mortals to hear a voice coming from the overgrown bushes in our backyards, see a message in the sun's rays, or have a visit from some minor angel, would it? Just imagine the fun—and the status we'd have telling others about our encounters with talking bushes, beams of light, and chats with mind-boggling extraterrestrial beings. Why, we'd be the envy of all those other Christians who hadn't experienced what we had. However ...

Check Your Bible, Not the Bushes

Much as we might wish for some spectacular visitation or lightning bolt experience to direct us, the fact remains: we need to check our Bibles to find out about being called. The Old Testament tells us that the Israelites were called to love God with all their being, serve Him by offering sacrifices, live according to the laws He gave, and care both for their own people and their slaves.

Calls to more specific tasks came to certain men and women whom God tapped to fulfill leadership roles as prophets, judges, or rulers. Where there were no written Scriptures or they were unavailable, God spoke through visions and dreams as well as other supernatural means.

Follow Me

At the beginning of His ministry, Jesus personally called Andrew and John as well as the other disciples to follow Him. That same call applies to every Christian. We needn't wait for a burning bush or a flash from the sky. We've already been called to serve—from deep within our hearts where God, the Holy Spirit lives.

When Jesus said, "Follow Me ... Whatever you did for one of the least of these brothers of mine, you did for me," and "Go and make disciples of all nations" (Matthew 4:19; 25:40; 28:19). He was speaking to all who would believe in Him down through the centuries. His call is to follow in His footsteps: carrying out His ministry of sharing the gospel; caring for the poor, downtrodden, and needy; and building up those who believe. We needn't wonder if this is His will or not—He's already told us it is.

Just as the early disciples were called to be with Him and serve under His direction, so are we. However, instead of hearing Christ's actual voice, we read His words. Instead of being instructed verbally on where to go and what to do, the Holy Spirit guides us through the Word. He also uses circumstances and the desires and gifts He puts within us.

There may be some mystical call to a special task—but in the meantime, there's plenty for every one of us to do for the Lord if we're willing.

Take a look around you. Is your neighbor or friend sick, lonely, depressed, or housebound? How can you show them God's love? Does your church have needs you could meet if you changed your priorities? Serving doesn't have to be an all-consuming task squeezed into an already exhausting schedule. It can be as quick as a five-minute phone call, grabbing a note card and scribbling down a verse you read that morning to cheer up a friend, asking someone over to share a light meal picked up from the deli, or having a perceptive word or helping hand for someone on a bus or in a store who looks sad, exhausted, or worried.

True, not every need is God's call to get involved. No one person can or should attempt to do everything. Nevertheless, knowing a person or ministry is in need obligates us to ask God if we are to help in some way.

Consider your present awareness of needs. Is there a person God wants you to serve, perhaps in a small way, or a ministry you could support? If He's bringing something to mind, write down how you might respond.

Pursue This Path

In addition to the general call we've all received—yes, sometimes God does lead us into a specific ministry. This call can come in several ways. We might find ourselves with a growing desire to serve in a particular way. If this desire has been implanted by the Holy Spirit, we'll find ourselves earnestly praying for God to bring it about. Often, however, God seasons us through a time of waiting.

Why does He make us wait when we long to get moving in a ministry? Because waiting and praying gives the Spirit time to search our hearts, revealing whether our longings are prompted by the flesh or by His Spirit. Waiting also tests our desire and our commitment, causing them either to diminish or become more intense. Then, one day, in God's timing, the door opens to what we've been longing for. We can hardly contain our joy to get started. God himself caused it to happen, and no matter what struggles we have in the road ahead, we'll always have the assurance that "God led me here and He will provide."

Another means God uses to draw us down a specific path of ministry is affirmation. What tasks do others frequently encourage you to take on? Do you enjoy the work involved? Are you repeatedly invited to serve in that way? These are clues to prayerfully consider.

When God's Word, input from mature Christians, prayer, and inner desire combine, perk up your ears, open your eyes, and look to see where God is leading you. "I will lead the blind by ways they have not known" (Isaiah 42:16).

When I resigned from teaching with Bible Study Fellowship, a friend gave me a hand-carved pen as a good-bye gift. On the enclosed card she wrote, "I believe writing is in your future." This was startling news to me. I'd never thought about it.

A year later a pastor friend asked when I was going to write what I teach. Still nothing registered. Another year passed and a published author, attending a Bible study I taught, asked if I'd ever thought about writing. Finally, I began to wonder if God was trying to say something. But it seemed so preposterous. Why would God call another person to write when there were plenty of able and eager writers everywhere?

At about this same time I read an article on the parable of the talents. Turning to Matthew 25, I mulled over Jesus' teaching. The principles seemed clear:

* *God has given each of His followers certain talents.* In Jesus' time, a talent was a sum of money. Today the word "talent" represents the resource or resources God gives us to serve Him. Without doubt, some receive more than others. Nevertheless, we all have some talent(s) from God to use for His purposes. Our joyful task is to discover what this is and then to use it for His glory.

* *God expects a return on what He's given us.* We can either waste or make good use of what God has given to us.

We can hide our talents—because we prefer to follow our own plans and priorities.

We can neglect our talents—because other things have greater priority in our lives.

We can bury our talents—because the risks and responsibilities seem too frightening.

* *God rewards those who put their talents to work.* In the parable, the master (God) said the same thing to two of his servants even though their achievements differed. God doesn't compare us with others, or rank us on some human scale of success. Rather, He looks at our service prompted by love for Him, and then says, "Well done, good and faithful servant." Notice something? The only servant who got blasted was the one who did absolutely nothing with what he'd been given. Could we have a more graphic reminder that God considers us responsible to make use of whatever abilities we have?

After thinking about the implications of this parable, I began to pray about the idea of writing. Was this a talent God had given that I'd never thought about? Was I willing to explore and see if this was true, risking failure and feeling foolish for trying? Was I willing to take time from other interests to pursue this new direction? Did I want to discover in eternity, too late, that God had given me certain gifts for serving Him but I had hidden from them, neglected them, or buried them? My answer to the last question was a fervent, "No, Lord!" And so I began, not having any thought of where it would lead, to move along the path toward becoming a writer.

Think about your own experience of serving God. What prompted you to go down a certain path—a desire to serve, a need, guilt, someone's encouragement, a Scripture verse, an inner longing? Record how God led you.

What has been the result in your life, and the lives of others?

I'm Equipped. But With What?

I've often wondered why God didn't limit mothering to those over forty. Mid-life women come equipped for the vital role of shaping the destiny of the next generation. They know who they are. They're self-controlled, kind, loving, and wise (well, at least some of the time). Of course, they probably lack the zip of moms in their twenties. But exactly how many of us who bore our offspring at a young age felt equipped for that task? Not I.

It's easy for us to feel just as ill-equipped to serve God. Haven't you ever thought, *Surely there's someone older, wiser, and kinder who could be called? There have to be others who have more to offer than I do.* What are we doing when we have these little conversations with ourselves? We're looking at our own resources and deciding whether to serve based on what we see, an instinctive impulse but one of our biggest mistakes.

If we look at ourselves, many of us will never feel adequate for what God calls us to do. Guess what? We're right. Our resources *aren't* sufficient, because God never intended us to do His work depending on our own abilities. So let's just forget what we have or haven't got going for us and change our focus. The truth we need to know and rely on is "It is God who works in you to will and to act according to his good purpose" (Philippians 2:13). If He calls us, He'll equip us—that's what He promises. Let's see how this works.

Equipped by Christ's Indwelling

Hudson Taylor, the great missionary to China, no doubt came across many Christians who felt totally inadequate to serve God. If you feel this way, reflect on his penetrating words:

> Many Christians estimate difficulties in the light of their own resources and thus they attempt very little, and they always fail.

> All giants have been weak people who did great things for God because they reckoned on His power and His presence to be with them.

More important than spiritual gifts, training classes, high energy, passion, or personality, is grasping the truth of Jesus' clear teaching on effective service. "No branch can bear fruit by itself; it must remain in the vine. Neither can you bear fruit unless you remain in me.... Apart from me you can do nothing" (John 15:4-5).

Depending on the Lord for power to serve Him effectively is the secret of bearing much fruit for God's glory. When this sinks in, we might still feel inadequately prepared, poorly trained, or incapable of being effective in our own power, but at least we know God is with us. The results are up to Him. What a relief. Now, instead of sending up silent, panicky prayers of protest, *God, what are You doing? You know I haven't a clue how to deal with this situation,* we can cheerfully pray, *Okay, Lord. You've put me in one of these impossible situations again. I can't handle it but I'm counting on Your power and presence to make me adequate. Here we go.*

When we're dependent on Christ's power and presence, we become His arms to comfort or provide help, His feet to go walking with a needy neighbor, His ears to listen to the brokenhearted. He uses our bodies to convey His love, truth, and wisdom. Whether those we serve are helped or changed is not a burden we're to carry—that's up to God. We're called to be available, to count on His resources instead of our own, and to relax in His assurance, "You did not choose me, but I chose you and *appointed you to go and bear fruit*—fruit that will last" (John 15:16, emphasis added).

Equipped by Spiritual Gifts

In addition to Christ indwelling us as our source of power to serve, we're also equipped by the Holy Spirit for the unique role He wants us to play in His body, the church. Serving God is often exciting and stretching, but when we actually discover where we fit, there's a sense of "I've found it. This is what You made me for, God. I love doing this."

The Olympic runner Eric Liddell, featured in the movie *Chariots of Fire*, was once asked why he ran. He replied, "Because when I run, I feel God's pleasure." Wouldn't you like to feel God's pleasure when you serve Him? To rise above gritting your teeth and saying, "All right, I'll help out," because you feel guilty or obligated? Don't you long to taste the deep satisfaction of serving God in a place where you fit? This can be your experience.

Shortly before going to the Cross, Jesus prayed, "I have brought you glory on earth by completing the work you gave me to do" (John 17:4). Jesus' goal was to do what the Father had called Him to do. This was the source of His joy. Can this be true for us, too? Absolutely. Discovering where we fit in and then getting into the action allows God to radiate our lives with joy, satisfaction, and purpose. But for this to happen, we first need to understand some biblical principles regarding spiritual gifts. In chapter twelve of his first letter to the Corinthians, Paul addressed this topic in detail.

Gifts come from the Spirit (vv. 4-7). When we became believers, we were placed in Christ and the Spirit of God came to live in us (Romans 8:1-9). He then gave us special capabilities through which we serve His church. This doesn't mean we can get along without various forms of training, however. To be as effective as possible, we can all profit from taking classes or seminars, reading books, listening to tapes, or just pitching in and getting hands-on experience.

Spiritual gifts are not the same as human abilities inherited from our personal gene pool, nor are they the result of education, our personalities, or skills we've acquired. They are gifts chosen for us *by the Spirit*. We don't get to pick them, nor are they something we attain through our own efforts.

We're all on God's gift list (vv. 4-31). No Christian is left without a gift. Everyone receives some divinely chosen ability from the Holy Spirit. In a local church, several might have the gift of leadership, but how it is expressed will vary according to what we feel passionate about.

Terry has the ability to lead others. She's able to get people organized, steering them in a direction that accomplishes a needed goal. Her buddy Lara has the same gifts. Do they necessarily work in the same area? No. "There are different kinds of service ... different kinds of working" (vv. 5-6). Terry's heart burns for the young moms program. Lara thrives in her church's inner-city ministry.

Our gifts motivate us to action, but how we express them can change with circumstances or different seasons of life. A gift of encouragement might motivate us to sponsor the youth group when we're in our twenties. Years later, this gift could be expressed through leading a support group. Our mode of serving might change over the years, but our gifts still shine through.

We all get personal attention. Every Christian is given spiritual gifts, but that doesn't mean we're all handed the same package. God is able to see us as individuals: He bestows gifts for special purposes. For instance:

Marcie is a great teacher—she loves to dig into background information, gather facts, and present her material in a systematic way. Put her in a room with a depressed woman, however, and she might pepper the poor lady with questions, expect logical answers, and briskly suggest that she "just apply this verse and your problems will be over." Jamie, a more empathetic sort, can often be seen giving a hug, listening, or quietly praying with another woman.

The body needs all the gifts. From inquisitive, sharp teachers, to those able to counsel compassionately, creatively decorate for special events, or cook for crowds of hungry people. Every person has a part to play; we complement one another. It follows, then, that we should be praising God for equipping the church so abundantly. Through the gifts given to each of us, He has provided the means to meet every conceivable need.

As His children, we haven't been treated like company employees who line up at the annual Christmas party to receive the same gift that everyone else gets. Knowing each of us personally, God decided which particular strengths we should receive so we can contribute through our unique place in the body.

Let this truth sink in and you'll be set free from thinking how inferior or inadequate you are. In truth, you'll experience a growing confidence. Try saying to the Lord and to yourself, *God, You have given me some gifts with which to serve You. The Bible says it, and I believe it by the witness of Your Spirit who lives within me.* If you find this hard to say, try it again. Every time you repeat this true statement, you please God by affirming exactly what He's told you in His Word.

Discovering Your Giftedness

Now that you've tossed out the idea that the Holy Spirit forgot all about you, it's time to discover what gifts you do have. In her helpful book *Giftedness, Discovering Your Areas of Strength*, author Marcia Mitchell describes several of the major gifts mentioned in Scripture. "You can know where you belong. You can find out exactly where you fit," she promises, providing a useful questionnaire to help you do just that.[3]

Many excellent tools are available to help you accurately pinpoint where your God-given abilities lie.[4] If you've never taken a spiritual gifts inventory, check with your church staff or inquire at your local Christian bookstore. You'll not only have fun completing these no-fail tests, you'll find yourself saying, "Oh, now I see why I like doing that, and why getting involved in that other area is the last thing I want to do."

Enlightening as these tools can be, discovering where to serve is *not* dependent on answering questions or analyzing what we've done or our personality type. Human resources are helpful but not essential. What is? Prayer, and a quiet listening for God speaking to our hearts and directing our path.

However you discover where your gifts and interests lie, remember, God designed you to be *you*. You honor Him when you celebrate your uniqueness, accept who you are, and serve in just the way He designed you to function. Like every member of Christ's body, you have something important to contribute—you might be a little finger, perhaps a hand, or even an arm. But whatever part you've been given to play, forget about measuring yourself against someone else. God thinks you're great. He sees your role as important. And He made *you* to glorify Him by just being you.

If you want to take spiritual strides, to grow in your experience of God's reality, tell Him you're available. Then watch to see how He leads you into exciting opportunities to serve and grow.

You and I might not be "super-saints" in our own eyes, but in God's eyes we are super-special and super-loved. He knows what He is doing in us, why He allows our struggles, and that spiritual transformation is happening even when we can't see it. He has promised to complete what He began in us. Even though we struggle with becoming the kind of Christians we long to be, let's joyfully declare, "Lord, continue Your work. I know You're not finished with me yet. When I trip up, help me get up. When I despair over my weaknesses, show me how to grow and change. Help me become what I so deeply desire—a woman after Your own heart."

Reflections—for Thought and Discussion

1. Have you ever found yourself thinking, *God couldn't use me!* What were your reasons?

2. What was your reaction to the list of people called by God to serve Him? Do any of them remind you of yourself? How does this encourage you to get involved?

3. Recall what it cost Jesus Christ to serve you. Then ask yourself, "What has it cost me to serve Him?" How does this question and the parable of the talents challenge you?

4. What do you feel God has called you to do for Him? If you don't know, is there something you particularly enjoy doing that meets needs? What is it?

5. Read the following references, looking for key truths about spiritual gifts: Romans 12:3-8; 1 Corinthians 12:12-27; 13:1-3; 1 Peter 4:10-11. What stood out to you from these verses and the section *Equipped by Spiritual Gifts*?

6. Try to think of the many ways God has rewarded you for being available to Him. Has He given you joy, fulfillment, respect, purpose—what else comes to mind? Take a moment to stop and praise God as you consider the great privilege we each have to serve the Sovereign, Eternal Lord.

Memory Verse

"Whoever serves me must follow me; and where I am, my servant also will be. My Father will honor the one who serves me" (John 12:26).

Notes:

1 Ray Beeson and Ranelda Mack Hunsicker, *The Hidden Price of Greatness* (Wheaton, Ill.: Tyndale House Publishers, Inc., 1985), 105-16. See also, Catherine Swift, *Gladys Aylward* (Minneapolis: Bethany House Publishers, 1984, 1989).

2 Bill Hybels and Mark Mittelberg, *Becoming a Contagious Christian* (Grand Rapids, Mich.: Zondervan Publishing House, 1994), 68-69.

3 Marcia Mitchell, *Giftedness, Discovering Your Areas of Strength* (Minneapolis: Bethany House Publishers, 1988), 11.

4 Jane A.G. Kise, David Stark, Sandra Krebs Hirsh, *LifeKeys* (Minneapolis: Bethany House Publishers, 1996).

END NOTES

Chapter Two

1 Hannah Hurnard, *Hind's Feet on High Places* (Wheaton, Ill.: Tyndale House, 1988).

2 Willard Erickson, *Christian Theology* (Grand Rapids, Mich.: Baker Book House, 1983), 952.

3 John Stott, *The Cross of Christ* (Leicester, England: InterVarsity Press, 1986), 148.

4 John Ortberg, *The Life You've Always Wanted* (Grand Rapids, Mich.: Zondervan, 1997), 17.

Chapter Three

1 From an article in *Straits Times*, Singapore (March 1998).

2 Richard Foster, *Celebration of Discipline* (San Francisco: HarperCollins Publishers, 1988), revised edition, 1-11.

3 From an article in *Straits Times*, Singapore (March 1998).

4 John Stott, *The Cross of Christ* (Leicester, England: InterVarsity Press, 1986), 64.

Chapter Four

1 John Piper, *Let the Nations Be Glad* (Grand Rapids, Mich.: Baker Books, 1993), 41.

Chapter Five

1 Richard A. Swenson, *Margins: Restoring Emotional, Physical, Financial, and Time Reserves to Overloaded Lives* (Colorado Springs, Colo.: NavPress, 1992), 222-223.

2 Charles Hummel, *Tyranny of the Urgent* (Downers Grove, Ill.: InterVarsity Press, 1967).

Chapter Six

1 Elizabeth George, *Loving God With All Your Mind* (Eugene, Ore.: Harvest House Publishers, 1994), 14.

2 Neil Anderson, *The Bondage Breaker* (Eugene, Ore.: Harvest House Publishers, 1990), 52.

3 Kenneth L. Barker and John R. Kohlenberger III, *NIV Bible Commentary, Volume 2: New Testament* (Grand Rapids, Mich.: Zondervan Publishing House, 1994), 19.

Chapter Seven

1 J. Oswald Sanders, *In Pursuit of Maturity* (Grand Rapids, Mich.: Zondervan Publishing House, 1986), 106.

2 Shere Hite, quoted in *The Sunday Oregonian* (October 18, 1987).

3 Jerry Bridges, *The Practice of Godliness* (Colorado Springs, Colo.:NavPress, 1983), 207.

4 Oswald Chambers, *My Utmost for His Highest* (Grand Rapids, Mich.: Discovery House Publishers, RBC Ministries, 1995), July 11 entry.

5 Jerry Bridges, *The Practice of Godliness*, 106.

6 Westminster Catechism.

Chapter Eight

1 John Stott, *The Cross of Christ* (Leicester, England: InterVarsity Press, 1986), 312.

2 Vernon Grounds, "Do All Things Really Work Together for Good?" (seminary handout).

3 Ibid.

4 Gerald Sittser, *A Grace Disguised: How the Soul Grows Through Loss* (Grand Rapids, Mich.: Zondervan Publishing House, 1997).

5 Rebecca Stowe, "Friends as Healers," *Modern Maturity* (Sept.-Oct. 1997).

Chapter Nine

1 Erwin Lutzer, *How to Say No to a Stubborn Habit* (Wheaton, Ill.: Victor Books, 1979), 50.

2 Charles R. Swindoll, *Three Steps Forward, Two Steps Back* (Nashville: Thomas Nelson Publishers, 1980), 99.

Chapter Eleven

1 Ray Beeson and Ranelda Mack Hunsicker, *The Hidden Price of Greatness* (Wheaton, Ill.: Tyndale House Publishers, Inc., 1985), 105-16. See also, Catherine Swift, *Gladys Aylward* (Minneapolis: Bethany House Publishers, 1984, 1989).

2 Bill Hybels and Mark Mittelberg, *Becoming a Contagious Christian* (Grand Rapids, Mich.: Zondervan Publishing House, 1994), 68-69.

3 Marcia Mitchell, *Giftedness, Discovering Your Areas of Strength* (Minneapolis: Bethany House Publishers, 1988), 11.

4 Jane A.G. Kise, David Stark, Sandra Krebs Hirsh, *LifeKeys* (Minneapolis: Bethany House Publishers, 1996).

About the Author

POPPY SMITH is the author of *I'm Too Young to Be This Old* and other books. For many years she was a Bible Study Fellowship lecturer and is a popular speaker at retreats, conferences, and workshops around the world. Born in England, she has lived in Sri Lanka, Singapore, and Kenya, where she met her American physician husband. They have two grown children.

To reach Poppy Smith regarding a speaking engagement, or to read more about her ministry, please visit her website:

www.poppysmith.com

Thank you to my friends who prayed me through this project. In particular, my grateful thanks to Karen Robbins, whose e-mails, cards, and phone calls from the other side of the world helped me to persevere. God also provided Suzanne Wells and Tamara Kitchen to critique, correct, and encourage. Your help was invaluable.

My daily prayer has been that God would use this book to teach and uplift women like myself, the non-"super-saints." If this is the result, may the glory go to Him alone

Made in the USA
San Bernardino, CA
30 March 2016